WALKING *on*
EGGSHELLS

WALKING *on* EGGSHELLS

Discovering Strength and Courage Amid Chaos

LYSSA CHAPMAN

with Lisa Wysocky

HOWARD BOOKS
New York   London   Toronto   Sydney   New Delhi

HOWARD BOOKS

An Imprint of Simon & Schuster, Inc.
1230 Avenue of the Americas
New York, NY 10020

First Howard Books trade paperback edition September 2018

HOWARD and colophon are trademarks of Simon & Schuster, Inc.

For information about special discounts for bulk purchases, please contact Simon & Schuster Special Sales at 1-866-506-1949 or business@simonandschuster.com.

The Simon & Schuster Speakers Bureau can bring authors to your live event. For more information or to book an event, contact the Simon & Schuster Speakers Bureau at 1-866-248-3049 or visit our website at www.simonspeakers.com.

Manufactured in the United States of America

10 9 8 7 6 5 4 3 2 1

The Library of Congress has cataloged the hardcover edition as follows:
Chapman, Lyssa.
Walking on eggshells : discovering strength and courage amid chaos / Lyssa Chapman with Lisa Wysocky. —First Howard Books hardcover edition.
pages   cm
1. Chapman, Lyssa, 1987– 2. Chapman, Duane (Duane Lee)—Family. 3. Dysfunctional families—United States—Biography. 4. Teenage mothers—United States—Biography. 5. Drug addicts—Rehabilitation—United States—Biography. 6. Television personalities—United States—Biography. I. Wysocky, Lisa, 1957– II. Title.
CT275.C482A3 2013
362.29092—dc23   2012036232
[B]

ISBN 978-1-4516-9608-0
ISBN 978-1-4516-9611-0 (pbk)
ISBN 978-1-4516-9615-8 (ebook)

To all my brothers and sisters
here on earth and in heaven.
I love you all.

No one born of God makes a practice of sinning,
for God's seed abides in him, and he cannot keep
on sinning because he has been born of God.

JOHN 3:9

Contents

Contents

Acknowledgments

Lyssa Chapman:

First and foremost I thank God for all I have been given. Many thanks also to my coauthor, Lisa Wysocky. You have become my voice in the dark and I'm so thankful for all you have done for me. To my literary agent, Sharlene Martin, I give my deepest gratitude. I am now her "daughter from another mother."

Huge thanks also to the many people who and organizations that helped me in so many important ways along my journey. These include, but are not limited to: Kerri Frazier, my councilor from school; Family Focus housing; Alysin, Aryn, and Nila Hauptner; Delorese Greigoir; Winners Camp, Hawai'i Leadership Academy; and Verna White.

Photographer Casandra Campeas, Anthony (her assistant), and Kokeeta Douglas, makeup artist, made my cover shoot fun. Thanks also to all my friends at Hybrid Films and D&D

Acknowledgments

Productions, Kimber Eastwood, Michele Maytum, Karen McKay Hennessy, Brenna Thiessen, and to Dad, Mom, and Beth.

Finally, thanks to everyone at Howard Books. I am very so excited to be working with you.

Lisa Wysocky:

*L*yssa Chapman has lived one of the most incredible stories of resilience that I have ever known. Even more amazing, she dug deep within to pull herself out of truly dire circumstances and made a better life for herself and her children. She is a remarkable young woman and is a bright, witty, compassionate, and totally fun writing partner. I am extremely honored to have written this book with her.

Many thanks to Lyssa's family for confirming dates and details of her childhood (and for providing photos), including Duane Chapman, Beth Chapman, Lyssa Greene, Tucker Chapman, Paula Hammond, Grace Katie Worthington, Leland Chapman, and Duane Lee Chapman.

I'd also like to thank the "world's best literary agent," Sharlene Martin of Martin Literary Management, and the entire team at Simon & Schuster/Howard Books, including Jonathan Merkh, Becky Nesbitt, Bruce Gore, Jennifer Smith, Felice Javit, and Amanda Demastus. This book obviously wouldn't "be" without any of you.

Finally, I'd like to thank you, the reader. Thank you for picking up this book. I hope that after reading Lyssa's story you will all look at life a little differently.

Introduction

When most little girls play house, they might imagine two happy parents with several well-behaved children, pretty rooms, flowers in the yard, and a white picket fence near the sidewalk. Me? I just wanted parents who could stand to be in the same room with each other.

You've probably seen me on television on the A&E hit reality program *Dog the Bounty Hunter.* I am Dog's daughter, Baby Lyssa. A lot of people think that Beth Chapman, Dad's wife, is my mom, but my dad and biological mother divorced before I entered kindergarten.

My life since then has been a roller coaster of highs and lows. Drugs and gang rape were interspersed with fun-filled trips to the beach with my family. Neglect, poverty, and teen pregnancy were balanced with my love for school. Racial hate crimes and sexual abuse were the norm one day, while joy and laughter filled the next.

As you may have seen on TV, my family is a complicated one. We often have strong differences of opinion and find ourselves at odds with one another. In particular I find that my relationship with my stepmother, Beth, is especially challenging. We are two very different people, but we make it work because the relationship is important to both of us.

In recent years I have also been able to see my dad as a person separate from him being my father. That's a perspective I think most grown children find eye-opening, and I am no exception here. My dad is not perfect, but no dad, no person, is. Dad has his own challenges, but I also know that he does the best he can— which usually is pretty darn good.

I hit rock bottom at the tender age of seventeen, an age when the biggest concern of most girls is the color of their prom dress. Instead, I was living in the cold Alaska climate in a car with my toddler daughter. I point no fingers here; that's just how life was. As a child, I so desperately wanted to grow up that I made many adult choices far before I was ready. Getting my life back together was a tremendous challenge, but it is by far the best thing I have ever done for myself and for my girls.

But I found that getting clean and sober, becoming a responsible parent, and pursuing a job that I love did not necessarily mean that life was all sunny. My beloved older sister, Barbara, was my best friend but she died tragically, far too young, in a car crash, and her death sent my world spinning. At twenty-one I married the man I thought was the love of my life only to find myself in an abusive situation. During all this I had been a regular on the show for several seasons and my life was an open book, open enough that I gave birth to my second daughter on camera in front of millions of people.

You might say that when I was young I was a kid who was out of control, and in many ways I was. I do take responsibility for all of my choices, good and bad. But I was also a child of neglect, a little girl with few boundaries or adults to guide me. Interestingly enough, from my youngest days I always knew that God had something better in store for me, that He had a better life waiting for me. And you know what? I was right!

Despite my challenges I look upon my life as a love story, for when all is said and done, I know that my mother and dad both love me and I love them. I love my daughters, my brothers and sisters, and the rest of my family, but I also love who I have become.

I have found the popular saying "If God brings you to it, He will bring you through it" so true, for I could not have gotten this far without His love and guidance. I can now proudly say that I embrace my life, all of it, and I look forward to helping guide other young women through their own troubled times. Keep reading and you'll learn all about it.

LYSSA CHAPMAN
January 2013

One

★

A Fairy Tale

*F*riday, February 20, 2009, was the most perfect day of my life. Not everyone gets to be married on national television on a beach in front of a beautiful Hawai'ian sunset. But I did. I was head over heels in love with my new husband, Brahman (Bo) Galanti, and more than two hundred friends and members of my extended family were there to support me.

On that day my family showered me with all the love I ever could have wished for. More than two hundred people showed up to celebrate as Bo and I exchanged the vows we had written. My wedding gown felt like something a princess would wear, and I was as giddy with excitement as any bride could be. When our family pastor, Tim Storey, pronounced us man and wife I was probably the happiest girl in the world.

Nothing could dampen my exuberant mood on my wedding day, not even the fact that I had made none of the decisions a bride usually makes. Choosing the flowers, invitations, and color scheme, even deciding on the kind of cake that was served—all of those decisions were made by my stepmother, Beth, and the production crew of my dad's reality TV series, *Dog the Bounty Hunter*. Normally I would have strong opinions about the details of my own wedding, but I was just so happy to marry the love of my life that I allowed Beth and A&E to make all of the decisions. They arranged for the wedding to be at Lanikohonua, a historical beachfront site in Ko Olina on the Hawai'ian island of Oahu.

My bouquet was a large fragrant mix of calla lilies and cascading blue flowers, and my dress was a gorgeous ivory silk by Demetrios with a plunging V-neck. Viewers of the show were probably unaware that I was fourteen weeks pregnant with my second child, as my dress was so well designed that it hid my small baby bump. I have made many mistakes in my life, and unmarried and unprotected sex were just two of them.

On my wedding day, however, I was thrilled about the idea of Bo and me parenting our new child together. All in all, I felt like I was in a fairy tale.

Fairy tales, however, are not all sweetness and light. They are riddled with darkness, just as my life has been. Snow White had to outsmart the evil queen. Little Red Riding Hood had to stand up to the big bad wolf, and Cinderella lived her formative years submitting to her oh so wicked stepsisters.

★

I was born Lyssa Rae Chapman II at General Hospital in Denver, Colorado, on June 10, 1987, a petite, blond-haired, green-eyed girl. I arrived at four forty-one A.M. and was named after my mother, Lyssa Rae Worthington Chapman. Lyssa, by the way, is pronounced as if it were spelled "Lisa." In her youth, my mother looked very much like a curly-haired Barbra Streisand. When she met Dad, she had graduated from Rama Bible College and was newly separated from her husband, who was a preacher. Apparently she and my dad fell in love immediately. They were married after my mother's first divorce was final in Estes Park, Colorado, on June 22, 1982, by an Indian chief who was also a judge.

My dad is Duane Lee Chapman, but you most likely know him as Dog the Bounty Hunter. There's not much in his life that has not been told. From the *Dog the Bounty Hunter* television show, which has aired internationally in more than twenty countries, to his bestselling books, to the hundreds of interviews and media reports, much of Dad's life is well known. Even though this is my story and not his, as Dog's daughter much of his story affected me, especially when I was living with him when I was a child.

My perspective, however, may not be what you expect.

I love my dad, but he is not perfect. No one is. We all do the best we can, and Dad has had his own challenges. In addition to fathering a dozen children, he has served time in prison for a murder he didn't commit, been a boxer, and been shot at more times than any of us can count. Now, as the "World's Most Famous Bounty Hunter," Dad has new hurdles in dealing with fame, a large family and staff, and in running several businesses.

Our relationship is beyond complicated, as is my relationship with my mother, but I love both of my parents more than words can say.

My early years were spent in Colorado, in a gang-infested neighborhood near Denver. I lived with my mother and dad in a run-down house that had been passed down through the family. There was graffiti on the cracked sidewalk and empty, burned-out houses across the street. With us lived my older sister and brother, Barbara and Tucker; my mother's son by her earlier marriage, Jason; and two of Dad's boys by one of his earlier marriages, Duane Lee and Leland. With six kids and a tiny house, we were often running wild out on the street. Everyone in the neighborhood knew we were Dog's kids, however, so the gang members who loitered on our street didn't mess with us. Even then, Dad was tough.

As the youngest child in this unusual household, I don't remember much. I know I was carried a lot, and being held in the arms of my family members went a long way toward making me feel safe in a drug-infested neighborhood. I have been told that my mother and dad fought a lot. Tensions in our family ran high when bills came due and there was no money to pay. Plus, Dad was often out doing bail bonds or bounty hunting, so care for all six of us was mostly left to our mother.

With half a dozen children and not enough money to go around, anyone would be overwhelmed. That was my mother. She loved to party, and from the time I was very young I knew she drank. I learned very early in life that there is a huge difference between partying and actually going to a party. My mother had a lot to escape from, and during this time in her life alcohol was her diversion. Today she might have joined a support group, gone to counseling, or taken a yoga class, but back then she must have felt that alcohol was her only choice. Either that or the pull toward substance abuse overcame the need to find a healthier alternative.

When I was small I adored my older siblings, especially my sister, Barbara. She was almost exactly five years older than I was—her birthday was June 8 and mine was June 10, and we used to have combined birthday parties on the ninth that I looked forward to for months. Everyone came: family, neighbors, and friends. And though a lot of kids were there, I knew I was Daddy's girl. Even through the roughest of times, I have always felt a special bond with my dad. I was his Baby Lyssa.

Dad wasn't always there, however. Work kept him away a lot, and to be honest, tension at home probably did, too. Because of that, and because my mother was so overwhelmed, Barbara became a surrogate mom to me. As far back as I can remember I looked to Barbara for help and guidance. When we were still living with both of our parents, Barbara was often the one who made sure

I had something to eat, who made sure I wore clothes that were at least somewhat clean, who comforted me at night when I'd had a nightmare. We were inseparable and I loved her with all my heart.

When I think about it I am amazed. Barbara at the time was just seven or eight. I look at my daughters, especially my older daughter, Abbie, who is nine as of this writing, and shudder to think of this beautiful little girl having to shoulder the responsibility that Barbara had at the same age. An old adage says that adversity makes you stronger, but sometimes I feel that too much of it just wears you down. Despite Dad's best efforts, the Chapman family in the late 1980s and early 1990s was just that: worn down.

A marriage is hard to hold together in the best of circumstances. Eventually the constant poverty—and the fighting it caused— drove my parents apart. I can now also speculate on the effects of alcohol and drug use, and of marital infidelity. From what I can see, everything stemmed from the choices of whether to use drugs and alcohol, and whether to fight. I also sometimes wonder how many different kinds of mental illness, such as depression or bipolar disorder, have affected various members of my family and how much they have contributed toward our dysfunction and addiction.

Today I see my parents as two different people with different goals and aspirations. But all I knew then was that "Mom and Dad" had come to the end of their marriage. When I was two, my mother left us to move in with her mother and care for her ailing stepdad. Barbara, Tucker, and I stayed with Dad. Barbara and Tucker cried a lot for our mother after she left but I'd always had so many people around that I didn't understand the concept of *mother*. I also didn't understand the idea that a permanent split between two adults meant that one of them wasn't coming back.

It wasn't long before Dad moved Tawny Marie, his secretary and new girlfriend, into the house with all of us. I remember only bits and pieces of the separation and eventual divorce, but I remember liking Tawny, who eventually married my dad. Tawny was the one who served my mother divorce papers from my dad, even though I am not sure why my mother was at our house. It could be that she had dropped us off after a visitation. I'm also not sure what my dad was thinking, especially as I can't imagine Dad doing it to deliberately hurt my mother. Maybe Tawny took it upon herself to fulfill the service so as to speed Dad's divorce along. Or Dad may have been thinking of Tawny in her role as his secretary. Since Dad was in the business of bail bonds and knew how our intricate legal system works, he might have decided to have Tawny serve the papers so he could save money on a process server. Something like the plumber fixing his own sink. Do it yourself so you know it has been done right. My parents were divorced on November 20, 1991. I was four years old.

My strongest memory of that time, however, was the day my mother and Tawny got into a terrible brawl and knocked each other around as if they were bowling pins. Again, I am not sure why they were together, but it was essentially a bar fight. By the time they began pulling each other's hair out, I had become hysterical.

This violent behavior from the two women who were supposed to take care of me was terrible to witness. From them I learned that the way to solve problems was through disrespectful name-calling and, if that failed, physical violence.

Today I am twenty-five, and understand that, as a young child, I was given little guidance. I don't mean to say that my parents didn't love me. I know they did, even though when I was small I wasn't always sure of it.

★

In the fall of 1992, when I was five, I started kindergarten and quickly came to love everything about going to school. Everything. Tawny always walked us to school, and in previous years we would drop Barbara and Tucker off, then Tawny and I would walk home. This year, however, I got to stay!

I loved meeting all the kids and making new friends, including my teacher, Mrs. Fox. Every day we had snack time, play time, and nap time, and I enjoyed the process of learning far more than you might imagine—especially for a girl with my particular family situation. For me, school was a safe place, an environment where I could be "normal," and it was a place where no one knew of my troubles at home. I could even, for a few hours during the school day, forget about all the tension within my family.

Even then I had a vague awareness that other parents thought about Dad and Tawny differently than they regarded parents of most of my classmates—Dad's career, the way our family was configured, even how my dad looked made him unique. When I was young, Dad had long hair worn in a kind of flattop mullet and was clean-cut. He was thin and so handsome that many of the other moms whistled at him. Plus, his suave, charismatic personality, combined with a crisp white shirt and black vest, made him impossible not to notice. Even though he was not yet a celebrity, there was never a time when he was shy and retiring. He has always known how to fill a room, even if he's the only one in it. That's also one of the many things I love about him.

I don't know how blatant his drug use was at that time, but I do remember seeing drug paraphernalia around our home. I didn't realize what it was or what the connotations could be—for me, it was just something else to wonder about, among all those other adult things that didn't seem to have much to do with me.

Because my mother left when I was so young I didn't have any strong memories of her. To be honest, I didn't even think about her much. Tawny was the first of half a dozen or more women Dad would eventually wind up having close relations with—women who each lived with us at one time or another. I wasn't really aware of the concept of a biological mother, so I called each of those women "Mom." It seemed natural, since to me "Mom" was simply any lady we lived with for a length of time and who took care of us.

Sometimes Dad had two women he saw regularly at the same time. That became a big thing for me to wonder about. For example, for most of the time Dad was married to Tawny, he was also pursuing other women, including Beth Smith, who later would become another of my stepmothers. Beth is Dad's current wife and starred along with Dad, two of my brothers, and me in *Dog the Bounty Hunter*. Beth first came into Dad's life when I was two, about the same time my biological mother left. When the divorce came through and Dad married Tawny, Beth was still an on-and-off presence.

Dad initially met Beth when he bailed her out of jail for shoplifting and illegal possession of a firearm. Then Beth and Tawny became good friends. I remember several times when Beth came to our house when I was very young, including the Christmas after Dad and my mother separated. This was unusual, as other women rarely hung out at our house. Over the years the relationship between Dad and Beth grew until even a child as young as I could see that there was more than friendship going on.

This is why I became confused about the roles of women in the home and in society. When you have never experienced normal, it is hard to recognize it when you finally find it. The same holds true for an abnormal life. For example, when your parents are continually high, it is hard to think of that as being either a bad or an unusual thing. I just regarded it as being "what grown-ups do."

As young as I was, I could see that Dad was making an effort to create a "normal" life for us, and even though he and Tawny fought just as my mother had fought with Dad, life was better when he stayed away from the partying lifestyle. During those times we went to church regularly and Barbara, Tucker, and I were able to develop our interests. For me it was dance. I so loved going to dance class. Dad really did want to give us the childhood he never had.

One of the people who helped Dad grow in life was the motivational speaker and author Tony Robbins. Dad had been going to and speaking at his seminars for several years. Dad often spoke to Tony's audiences about his time in jail for a crime he didn't commit, and how much Tony's words and philosophy had helped him over the years. At about the time I turned six, Dad attended a ten-day Tony Robbins seminar in Hawai'i while our grandmother, Dad's mom, watched us. Dad and Tawny had been married only a little while, but already it was on-again, off-again.

Dad fell in love with Hawai'i and did not return home to us until our initial two-week stint with Grandma had turned into more than a month. When he did return, he happily announced that we were moving to the Aloha state. I was still at an age where I had no concept of the enormity of change this move was going to bring. But the plane ride, the endless ocean, and the new house in a tropical paradise all represented such great challenges that they made life feel strange and unreal, even for a little girl growing up in the surreal fashion that I was.

Still, even if all of my life challenges so far were combined, they would not come close to the test my elementary school years would prove to be.

Two

★

New Identity, New Life

*H*awai'i *truly is one* of the most beautiful places in the world, and I understand why Dad fell head over heels for it. I live on the island of Oahu, where the weather is perfect year-round and there is a lot to see and do. I love hiking and being able to take my kids to the beach every day. Between the beach, hiking up Koko Head (the headland that defines the eastern side of Maunalua Bay), the Makapu'u Lighthouse trails on Oahu's east side, and the many waterfalls, Hawai'i has it all. For me, it is home.

But even paradise isn't perfect. My move here when I was six taught me that people and life situations can mar what is otherwise ideal. For example, my brother Duane Lee did not move to Hawai'i with us. Instead, he chose to stay in Colorado with his girlfriend, and I missed him terribly. There were also many new things in my world, and most of my time was spent getting used to the warmer climate, the lush vegetation, and the unusual accents spoken by many of the people in Hawai'i.

Although English and Hawai'ian are the co-official languages of Hawai'i, I quickly learned that many Hawai'ian residents speak a broken form of English called Pidgin. Early Hawai'ian settlers and plantation workers influenced Pidgin by the many different languages they spoke. Eventually Pidgin was used outside the plantation, kids learned Pidgin from their classmates, and over time it became the primary language of most people in Hawai'i.

For a young, newly arrived Hawai'ian like me, Pidgin was very difficult to understand. For example, "th" sounds are replaced by "d" or "t" so *that* becomes *dat,* and *think* becomes *tink.* An "l" at the end of a word is often pronounced "o" so *people* becomes *peepo.* And an "r" after a vowel is often dropped, so *letter* becomes *letta.*

In addition, the intonation of Pidgin is much different from traditional American English. Instead of the tone of a person's voice rising at the end of a question, for example, as it does in English, in Pidgin, it drops. I couldn't understand most people when I got to Hawai'i, and I was soon to find that most people didn't understand me.

When it was time for me to start school, I became very excited. I had loved kindergarten and expected more of the same at my new school, President Thomas Jefferson Elementary School, just a few short blocks from the beach in beautiful Waikiki. I wasn't disappointed.

For school, Tawny made sure that Barbara, Tucker, and I dressed in clean, stylish clothes and that our hair was immaculate. Not every seven-year-old gets a perm, but I did. Other than having difficulty understanding people, life in Hawai'i that year was wonderful. Dad's bail bonds business was thriving, and we were living the dream.

On New Year's Eve that year Dad had a special treat for us. He rented a large, luxury car and we all piled in and drove down the main drag in Waikiki. Dad put the top down and pretended like we were the main attraction in a parade. He had that big Dad grin on his face and smiled and waved at everyone we passed. He even thought to buy a boatload of candy that we threw out to people. Dad knew how to make all of us feel special.

When we first moved to Hawai'i we all lived together in a studio apartment in downtown Honolulu in a high-rise complex called the Marina Surf. For several months Dad, Tawny, Tawny's daughter, Nikki (who was about Leland's age), Leland, Barbara, Tucker, and I all lived in that one room. All I remember about that place was how crowded it was. I was glad that as soon as he could afford it Dad moved us to a nearby two-bedroom apartment in the Waipuna complex on Ena Road in Waikiki.

That complex was very nice and had a swimming pool on the seventh floor. I remember Dad teaching me how to do a swan dive off the diving board there. There was also a huge koi pond on one side of the building, complete with gazebo, swans, lily pads, and frogs. The apartment manager used to pay Tucker and me a dollar for each frog we caught out of the koi pond and delivered to him. I remember getting up at six in the morning and going down to wade knee-deep through the pond in search of frogs. Tucker was a lot more successful at frog catching than I was.

Across the street from our new apartment was a seedy place called the Hostel. My dad and biological mother had been divorced for several years, but my mother had fallen on hard times and was pregnant, so Dad flew her from Colorado to Hawai'i and rented a room for her at the Hostel. It was a dirty, disgusting place then, and even today we bounty-hunt there a lot, so you can imagine the kind of people who lived there back then, but it may have been the only close place Dad could find or afford.

Visiting on weekends during this time gave me my first real memories of my mother. She would walk across the street to pick up Barbara, Tucker, and me, and the only thing Dad would say was, "Don't let them watch *Beavis and Butt-head*."

Beavis and Butt-head was an animated television series on MTV that featured two degenerate teenagers. It was totally unsuitable for three elementary school-age kids to watch, but of course that show was the first one we all turned on when we got to my mother's. I remember that she enjoyed the show as much as we did; it was a guilty pleasure for all of us.

I also remember playing in the large, covered courtyard. The

Hostel didn't have apartments per se, just studios with a kitchenette and bathroom, so some of the residents often sat in the courtyard in front of their rooms and socialized.

A few months after my mother arrived my little brother Nick was born. Even though Nick is technically my half brother, that term was never used in our family. We never used the word "step" either—not for grown-ups, and certainly not for sisters and brothers. But with all the blending of moms and siblings, we all knew that there was only one dad.

When Nick was a few months old, he and my mother moved back to Colorado, and it was several years before I saw her, or Nick, again.

★

During this time Dad and Tawny were still having marital problems, so after I finished school that year Tawny and all of us kids moved to the island of Hawai'i, also known as the Big Island. Tawny apparently knew someone there and could also write bail bonds for Dad without having the tensions of day-to-day togetherness.

Our new home was in Kailua-Kona, on the western coast of the island. At the time Kailua-Kona was quite rural. I was looking forward to a great year at my new school, Kealakehe Elementary, but I was in for a surprise. On my first day, I realized I was the only white kid there. As far as I could tell, all of the other kids were of Hawai'ian, Samoan, Filipino, Chinese, or Japanese descent—everything but Caucasian. Immediately I discovered I was an outsider. The other kids kept calling me "haole," which on the surface means white person, or foreigner. The word is also derived from *hā'ole*, meaning "no breath." Years ago, when foreigners to the island did not know to use the *honi*, a Polynesian greeting of touching nose-to-nose and inhaling or sharing each other's breath, some native Hawai'ians described them as breathless. The implication is not only that foreigners are aloof and ignorant of local ways, but also that they have no soul or life within. But on top of that, it was the derogatory way the word was said that made me feel so bad inside.

In Colorado I had friends of many colors, and the shade of a person's skin was not important to me. It never had been and still isn't. Here, however, the kids were teaching me that many people of Hawai'ian or islander descent were mean inside. It was a terrible lesson to learn. Fortunately, I have since found that is not true and have actually found native Hawai'ian and other island people to be some of the best people on the planet.

In second grade, though, I was terrified to go to school. When I walked into the building each morning I knew that during at least one point during the day one or more of my schoolmates would push me hard into the dirt. Then, at lunch, no one ever wanted to sit with me, "the white girl," so I either sat by myself or ate outside with a teacher. I felt so alone. No matter what the activity, the other kids excluded me, and this made me sad and insecure.

At recess we sometimes had organized activities, such as King of the Hill. Instead of a fair game, though, this was more like an open invitation to my classmates to pound me into the ground. At other times I stood at the edge of the playground and watched everyone else have fun. The swings were always full with children who were shrieking with joy, while other kids paired up to play tetherball, which was the hot thing back then. If I tried to participate, kids called me names, jeered, taunted me, and sometimes even punched me. Barbara and Tucker, who were old enough to be in middle school, received regular beatings for being white, so I guess I was lucky.

To make matters worse, it wasn't just the kids. In the classroom, my teachers, who I still had difficulty understanding, were mean to me as well. I clearly remember sitting in class one day when the teacher singled me out and put the blame on me for all the white people who stole Hawai'ian land more than a hundred years earlier. I was a seven-year-old child. I was no saint, but how could I possibly have been responsible for that? All of this combined to send me home every day in tears.

I soldiered on, however, and tried to find positive things to look forward to at school. Once we had a special day where we were going to play outside and eat traditional Hawai'ian food. I was particularly looking forward to trying *maunapua*—I wasn't sure what it was, but I had overheard some of the other kids talking about it as it if was a big treat. I couldn't wait to try it! I didn't know that maunapua is Pidgin for the Hawai'ian word *mea'ono-pua'a,* or pork cake—a warm patty of baked white bread filled with fatty pork meat. All the other kids thought it was wonderful, but it really was the most disgusting thing I had ever put into my mouth. It tasted terrible and I was so disappointed that my much-awaited treat turned out to be something I disliked that I cried and cried. My tears over the maunapua only proved to the other kids that yes, I really was weird.

At home I was able to let my feelings out fully. Tawny had always been very affectionate toward me, and I really loved her. Barbara also gave me advice, and I took a lot of solace from my dolls. As early as I can remember I loved playing with dolls. I'd dress them up for tea parties, rock their babies, and give them all the love I could. It was a nice, safe distraction from the anxious hours I spent at school.

I also loved going to church and listening to Pastor Jeremiah Hoaeae preach. While Dad rarely, if ever, went to services, he made sure all of his kids were there every Sunday morning. And even though I was far younger than the other kids, I had been on many retreats with this church's youth group. On Sunday morning I was always the lucky girl who was trusted to change word sheets on the projection screen for the opening songs of worship. Unlike school, at church I felt accepted.

School life finally delivered me a gift, though. One day out of the blue, a large Samoan girl in my class named Emma sat down next to me and we became friends. I have no idea why she chose to sit by me, or why she reached out to befriend me, but I cannot express what her friendship meant to me. It was everything.

After Emma and I became friends she protected me from my classmates, and my fear of being beaten and ridiculed lessened. I now had a partner to play tetherball with and someone to sit with at lunch. In class, when we paired up for projects, I was no longer the last chosen or the odd person out. Instead, Emma's eyes would meet mine, and in that secret language of togetherness we'd silently agree to work as a team. Life after Emma was so much better. I had an ally, a friend. When we moved away a year or so later I lost touch with Emma, so, girl, if you are reading this, please contact me! I'd love to reconnect with you.

At about this same time Tawny hooked up with people she shouldn't have, and they were a bad influence on her. At this point life slowly began a descent that would take me ten years to pull out of.

The first big change this brought into my life began the day of a parent-teacher conference. The morning of the conference I made sure my school desk was tidy and all my papers were neatly aligned. Tawny was going to meet with my teacher that afternoon, and I knew how much Tawny would appreciate my clean desk. I loved Tawny and wanted her to be proud of me. But when I got home after our early dismissal, Tawny was backing out of our driveway with Nikki and all of their clothes in the car.

"Wait," I called to her. "You *are* going to my conference, aren't you?" I asked.

"Yes, sweetie," Tawny replied. "I will be there." Of course she didn't go, and I only remember seeing her twice after that.

Leland, who was by then about twenty, picked up the slack, but it wasn't until a week later that he called Dad to tell him that Tawny had left. The delay was due to the fact that Tawny had implied to him that her absence was going to be temporary. But after a week with no word, Leland knew that Tawny was gone for good.

★

I was too young to know what Dad's reaction was to Tawny's departure, but he did his best and dug in to keep things as normal for us as possible. To do that he hired a woman I'll call Deanna as our nanny. I soon came to love Deanna as if she were another older sister.

I also quickly realized that Deanna had a thing for my dad. In fact, she was super crazy for him. Dad reciprocated, and my relationship with Deanna went, just like that, from pseudo-sister to "Mom" overnight. It happened on New Year's Eve after a fireworks display at a neighbor's. Dad and Deanna both got drunk, and before anyone realized what was happening they were in his bedroom. That was something else to add to my confusion about female role models.

Dad still spent most of his time in Honolulu, as the majority of his business was there. Because he was often away he probably didn't pick up on it, but as we got to know Deanna better we saw many things that indicated she could be a little off: her intensity, her manic laughter, her opinions that were a bit too strong. For example, she continually blasted music at beyond earsplitting levels. I also remember having a firecracker fight with her with little red firecrackers—inside the house. These were sides of her that I had not seen before. Nothing, however, prepared me for her to become unglued one day. One afternoon Deanna just went berserk. I have no idea why, but I can speculate that it was because of drug and alcohol use. I still remember her screaming, again and again and again. No words, just these loud, loud screams. I was terrified. I couldn't move. I couldn't breathe. Fortunately, either Tucker or Barbara called the police, and Dad flew home from Honolulu to rescue us.

To get Deanna out of the house, Dad arranged for her to be sent to the States. The earliest flight he could find for her, though, was several days away. So Dad got Deanna a room at a local hotel, and a police officer drove her there. Boom, no more nanny, but I was glad. Her intensity had made it hard for all of us to feel comfortable in our own home.

Dad next moved his parents, my grandma and grandpa, to the Big Island. Dad's dream was to bring all of his family over, and this was a big step toward that. Grandma and Grandpa had their own place near us, and we saw them just about every day. My grandma Barbara Darlene was a sweet, godly woman who had been a preacher back home on her Navajo reservation. I have many fond memories of listening to her stories and of coming home from school to her loving embrace. She created an idyllic home environment, and the turmoil of Tawny's split from our family and Deanna's craziness soon faded.

Unfortunately, my grandma passed away not too many months after she arrived. She and Grandpa had both smoked unfiltered Camel cigarettes since adolescence, and Grandma developed emphysema. Before she moved to Hawai'i she needed to use an oxygen tank, but for whatever reason, in Hawai'i her health improved enough so she didn't need the tank anymore. Or so we thought, because one night she went to sleep and never woke up. Grandma was just sixty-one.

Grandma had an open casket, and I remember being startled at seeing her body. It was the first dead body I'd ever seen. Pastor Jeremiah Hoaeae led the services, and he spoke about the body being a shell, that Grandma's soul was no longer in it. Her spirit had gone to a better place so we shouldn't mourn, he said. But I did. We all did.

At the service Leland's girlfriend did a beautiful hula dance. Tawny even came and shed tears. My grandpa had been a navy man and was a really tough guy. The entire event was beyond sad, but my grandpa was the most devastated of us all. Soon after, my grandfather returned home to Colorado. We all missed them both.

I loved my grandma deeply and I knew she loved me just as much. But we had to move on as a family. In the midst of his grief, Dad regrouped again. From his perspective, it must have been a terrible time. First his wife leaves him, then his mom passes away.

Dad adored his mother, and I know her loss left a huge void in his life. Dad also had a slew of young children to be responsible for and a business to run. That is a lot for anyone to handle. Before long some of the balls Dad was juggling so precariously began to drop. First, business fell off. Tawny had written a lot of bonds on the Big Island, and it was hard for Dad to keep up with two locations on two different islands. Next, some of his employees began to mismanage Dad's business. They must have thought that with Dad being so distracted he wouldn't notice, and I don't think he did—at first. But by the time he did it was almost too late to bail himself out of a huge financial hole.

Still, Dad spent as much time as he could with us. He set up a business line in our house, and all of the kids, myself included, began answering the bail bonds line to help out after school. Necessity is the mother of invention, and I soon became very good at giving instructions and taking messages over the phone. I can just imagine what Dad's clients must have thought when a seven-year-old regularly answered his bail bonds business line.

Leland also helped out by taking us to school. On weekends we all went on crazy adventures with Dad. We went fishing a lot, and I remember being in a boat with Dad and Leland, who were spear fishing. Both were bare-chested, and I can still remember how happy they were when one or the other actually speared something. Another time we sailed all the way to Captain Cook Point, and Dad told us how Captain Cook had discovered Hawai'i. During those trips I found that I really loved the ocean. There was something calming to me about the rhythm of the waves. I also loved swimming and asked Dad to take me every chance he got.

Dad often took time to read to us to from the Bible, and as a family we talked about what the stories meant. We had some great discussions. One day we learned that a local boy and girl had drowned tragically in a pool. Dad was so moved by the incident that he wrote a story about them. I vividly recall him reading his story to us and can picture Dad's handwriting on the blue paper that he ripped out of a notebook. He wrote that our grandma met the two children in heaven and grabbed their hands to welcome them.

To ensure that all of his children were safe and well cared for when he was away, Dad put an ad in the paper for a nanny. It wasn't long before a number of very pretty nannies moved, one by one, into our home, and then out. Even though I was quite young, it didn't take me too long to figure out what was happening. After a few days or weeks of taking care of us during the day (and at night when Dad was out of town), each nanny somehow began sleeping in Dad's room.

I can't tell you how many nannies we had. It seemed like dozens—but I am sure the number was far less than that. Of all the nannies, we had one in particular whom I became very fond of. Unlike the others, she was not classically beautiful. It turned out that the other nannies were ultimately there because Dad must have seemed quite a catch, but I could tell that this nanny was there for *us*. She kept our house spotless, cooked great meals, and every day when I came home the house smelled wonderful. Once she even served escargot, a French delicacy of cooked snails that I had never even heard of before.

This nanny meant so much to me. One evening I was sitting at the dinner table and when we bowed our heads before the meal I remember praying out loud, "Dear God, *please* don't let Dad screw the nanny." I wonder how many little girls are anxious about that particular topic. Several days later I woke up to find my beloved nanny sleepily coming out of Dad's bedroom, and I was heartbroken that God hadn't answered my prayer.

★

I'm not sure which of the nannies first turned Dad on to hard drugs. Or maybe it wasn't a nanny. Maybe it was someone else, but at about this same time Dad became more and more distracted, and business dropped off significantly. Dad, who had been our rock, was becoming irresponsible.

Toward the end of my second-grade year I was thrilled to be part of a talent show at school. I was going to dance to one of my favorite songs, "Dream Lover." I wasn't part of much of anything in the schoolroom, so the talent show was a rare opportunity for me to fit in.

Dad promised me he wouldn't miss this event for anything, and I couldn't wait to show off onstage for him. But during the performance, which was held during a daytime school assembly, I looked at every single person in the room and scanned every single face. I couldn't believe my dad was not there, but he wasn't. I was so disappointed. Later, at home, I asked Dad how he liked my performance—just to be sure I hadn't missed seeing him. His vague answer only confirmed my suspicion that he did not see me dance.

Second grade finally ended, and for my eighth birthday, Dad hired a clown. I excitedly sent out invitations to everyone in my class and to several neighbor children. When the big day arrived I was jumping up and down with anticipation, but my exhilaration soon turned into a black pit of anxiety that settled in the center of my stomach. Other than the clown, my friend, Emma, was the only one who showed up for the party. Dad was in his bedroom with the nanny du jour, and only came out of his room for a few minutes on my special day. I wish I had understood how badly Dad was hurting, and that the nannies and the drugs were his way of self-medicating his pain.

On my eighth birthday I felt terribly alone. I am not sure why the other invited children did not come to my party, although I can think of several reasons. Some parents might not have wanted their children to associate with me because they suspected that my dad used drugs. It might also have been that parents didn't want their kids associating with a "white girl." With Emma as my friend the racist attacks on me had lessened, but I still had to watch my back. It could also have been that kids still thought I was weird. I talked differently, I looked different, and I liked different foods. The gap just may have been too big for eight-year-olds to bridge. The result, however, was that I was devastated.

I entered third grade at yet another new school, Honuanua Elementary, which sat on top of a hill in the Big Island town of Captain Cook. When I was young, Dad had a habit of not renewing his rental agreements, so we moved a lot. This was my fourth school in four years and something like my fourth house in two years. I was getting good at adapting but did not have any more luck making friends in this school than I had at the previous one. Plus, I had lost Emma, my friend and protector, in the move so in some ways third grade was even worse than second grade had been.

★

In writing this book I found I had to make a choice. I could choose to skip over the really bad parts of my life, or I could be honest and share them. Not mentioning the bad experiences might keep a few readers from becoming offended, but it also would eliminate segments of my life that impacted me profoundly. After significant thought I decided I had to share; otherwise this account would not be honest. Not sharing might also make a few readers confused as to my behavior in my early teens, which were right around the corner. Here's the first of several really bad events in my life.

While Dad was otherwise occupied, my siblings were dealing in their own ways with the losses our family had endured. Leland was old enough that he could go out on his own and make his own life, but Barbara and Tucker were stuck at home with me. Their way of coping was to get into the Goth lifestyle. For my brother and sister, this meant dressing in black, wearing ghostly white makeup, dying their hair jet-black, experimenting with drugs, and hooking up with people of the opposite sex.

Barbara was only five years older than I was, which would put her at about thirteen. The age gap between us at that stage of our lives, however, was huge, especially as Barbara's friends were all a few years older than she was. It made finding things to do together difficult, as we were into very different activities.

My after-school hours became a nightmare. At first I spent that time alone in my room listening to music on my stereo. But what I really wanted to do was spend time with Barbara and Tucker. However, they often had friends over. On a typical afternoon, Dad would pop his head out of his room and instruct my siblings to play with me. Their version of that, though, was to allow two of their friends to make me watch as they messed around on the floor, which turned into the two friends having sex. My siblings also often stuck me in a closet in Barbara's room with a thirteen-inch TV/VCR combo and a pile of porn videos. On another occasion they made me watch as their friends killed a cat and drank the blood. This was during a time when my siblings Goth tendencies became overshadowed by devil worship. As much as I believe in God and in the power of good, I also believe in the devil and the evil that follows him. At this time in my life I learned that hard lesson.

I also loved animals, so the cat killing was especially traumatizing for me. I was very young and impressionable; at only eight years old all I wanted was to fit in. What I heard and saw during those afternoons gave me a totally unrealistic picture of life, love, and relationships.

Today I have gained enough perspective to understand that the dysfunction in which I grew up made it much harder for me to understand normal. I have just now begun to recognize and understand healthy relationships, but for me, I had to understand unhealthy first.

Three

★

Family Ties

Today I know where my children are at all times. As a child I got into my most serious trouble when I was unsupervised, which is why I keep such close tabs on my kids. If I lose sight of them, whether it is at the supermarket, the park, or the mall, I instantly panic and feel helpless and breathless until my eyes reach their adorable blond heads. The mere thought of being separated from them makes me petrified.

Even though my life at home was not as good as it could be when I was young, the thought of being separated from my family terrified me. I loved my family fiercely. We were like a gang, the Chapman Gang, and what stability and comfort I had in life came directly from them. But my greatest fear was to come true twice in the coming months.

By this time we had moved again. One day after school when Barbara and Tucker were still in their Goth phase, I found myself sitting on the floor in the center of a circle surrounded by my two siblings and their friends. What was most interesting to me, however, was that everyone took turns blowing smoke in my face from a joint they all shared. I got stoned right away, and I remember the good feeling I had when everyone laughed. I felt good not just because of the pot, but also because this particular kind of laughter, to me, meant acceptance.

I was so happy to be included in any activity my older brother and sister might initiate that I didn't give any thought to how appropriate the activity might—or might not—be. I could tell that Tucker wasn't too keen on me actually smoking pot myself, but his resolve lasted only a few days, and before I knew it, I had my own joint to keep me busy while I watched the porn videos in the closet.

Fortunately I also had other, more appropriate, avenues of entertainment. Dad has always been an animal lover, and we had lots of animals around when I was growing up. If we saw something cute, he let us bring it home. Pets are such friends, especially to little girls who don't have many companions. They are also great teachers.

I remember that Dad bought me a little lovebird that I named Rockadoodle. I loved this bird so much! He sat on my finger and I spent hours listening to him sing catchy tunes. One evening I decided to take my feathered friend to bed with me, and we snuggled down together.

When I awoke the next morning I found a lifeless little bird next to me, and I ran to my dad to share the news. Bless Dad for knowing the right thing to do for me at that time in my life— Dad took Rockadoodle and told me he would fix him. After what seemed like hours of waiting Dad told me Rockadoodle had made a full recovery but had decided to live in a big tree outside, rather than in a cage inside the house. Dad then took me to a window where we both looked out. Then he pointed to a large tree and told me that was where Rockadoodle now lived.

I now know that I probably rolled over in my sleep and squashed my little friend, but Dad never let me know that. While it might have been a wonderful "teachable moment" for another child, I had already suffered the loss of so many people whom I loved that Dad knew I didn't need to hear that about Rockadoodle.

★

At about this same time, with the departure of yet another nanny whose name I don't remember, I found that two new people had come into in my life. "Ginny" was our new nanny. And a man I'll call Nathan soon became a friend of my dad's. Nathan was a balding older man who became a sort of sensei to my dad. In addition to being a kind of spiritual teacher and a regular fixture in our household, Nathan also had a charismatic personality.

Ginny found us when she answered one of Dad's ads. She was a very nice, pretty girl who had a two-year-old son I'll call Andy.

The thing I remember most about Andy was that he was a really big kid for his age. The addition of Andy to our household was very exciting to me. Until this time, whatever configuration we had of family in our house, I was always the youngest. I was Baby Lyssa. That's why any person younger than I was a source of extreme interest and fascination.

Ginny didn't last long in her role as nanny before she was "upgraded" to dad's girlfriend. And from the beginning, Dad and Ginny's relationship was passionate, both physically and emotionally. As the weeks and months passed after Ginny was hired, Dad became less frequent and less present in our lives.

During this time Dad and I took a ride in his car and he began smoking a crack pipe like it was a cigarette. Dad has since said that, at the time, he had no idea what crack was. That maybe explains why when Dad first started smoking crack (from my perspective) he never tried to hide it. He thought it was the coolest, hippest thing in the world. It wasn't too long, however, before his new habit came to the attention of a few people who didn't think it was quite so cool.

One day during a DARE (Drug Abuse Resistance Education) class at school the teacher showed Tucker's class pictures of some drug paraphernalia. When the photo of a crack pipe came up, Tucker shouted out something to the effect of, "Hey, my dad uses one of those."

Twenty-four hours later, as the school day ended and I was standing on the second-floor balcony waiting for Dad to pick me up, several school officials came to escort me to a nearby room, where they told me I was not going home with Dad that day. Out the window, I watched my dad storm up the front stairs of the school, absolutely furious. Even from the second floor I could hear him yelling, but the result was that I was put into a car with strangers and taken to a Child Protective Services (CPS) office to a small room with a few books, waiting for I didn't know what.

You can imagine my fear and confusion. Here I was, an eight-year-old little girl, and all I knew was that I was being taken from my family. I didn't understand why. I didn't know why I had to be checked for bruises and such, or where we were going. Terror formed an icy ball deep inside me.

After everyone was done looking at me, I was again loaded into the car. Now I was told that we were going to a Taco Bell and then we'd drive all the way to the other side of the island so I could meet my new family. New family? What new family? I loved my old family! I wanted to go home to my dolls, to our house. I desperately wanted my dad.

After we stopped at the restaurant we went to a park so I could stretch my legs before the long drive ahead. They were taking me to Hilo, which was a two-and-a-half-hour drive. I think these strangers hoped I would burn off some energy at the park before the trip.

My "captors" were very careful not to leave me alone, but they made one huge mistake. In conversation, they mentioned that Tucker had also been taken from Dad but had escaped. I knew then that I had to do something, or I might never see my family again. In my mind, these people were kidnapping me, and I was afraid Dad would be mad at me for letting them do that. So as soon as their backs were turned, I ran.

I took off and ran as hard and as fast as I could and put as much distance as I could, as quickly as possible, between those other people and me. Fortunately, I was familiar with this park, as Dad had taken me there to play a number of times. I ran to the closest highway and an older couple picked me up in their ancient pickup truck. I am forever grateful to them. I sat between them in the front seat and asked to be dropped off at a McDonald's that I knew was up the street. They seemed happy to do so. Today I think that if anyone saw a small, panting, frightened, out-of-breath child on a street corner, they'd probably try to find out why the child was panicked. But like an answer to a prayer, a car showed up when I needed one and the driver drove me where I needed to go, no questions asked.

When I got to the McDonald's, I placed a collect call to my dad with trembling fingers. Many of Dad's bail clients called collect, so I knew what to do. I could hear the relief in Dad's voice as he told me to hide somewhere close by; I would be rescued as soon as possible. I have always been small and I found a perfect hiding place under a seat and waited. And waited.

My heart was thumping in my chest so hard that I was sure it would give me away. It seemed like forever, but Ginny eventually got there. Dad was afraid the police might be looking for him so he sent Ginny instead of coming himself.

That night I was so happy to be home, surrounded by people I loved. But my happiness was not to last very long. The next morning a pounding on the door awakened me. The police were there with Child Protective Services, and I realized that they wanted Barbara, Tucker, and me to leave with them.

"Over my dead body!" Dad shouted. "If you take them now, they will come back, just as they did yesterday."

If I ever doubted that Dad loved me, those fears were put to rest right then. Even I could see that this was a man who was doing his best to protect his family. I also have to admit that while most of my childhood memories are crystal clear, maybe because I was so traumatized by the event that here some of my memories are a bit foggy. My dad has a somewhat different recollection of the details of this time. However, the main facts remain clear to us both: CPS took me away from my family and I escaped.

On hindsight, I have to acknowledge that we were minor children living in a home where a parent was doing hard drugs. Should we have been removed from the home? It's an interesting question. I think that what my dad needed at this time more than anything was love, guidance, and support. It was about this same time that Tony Robbins stopped asking Dad to speak at his seminars, and I know how much that news must have hurt. I've often thought that if Dad had someone in his life who could have been there in person to give him support and encouragement daily, that life might have turned out differently for all the members of my family.

But then again, maybe not. Maybe the wheel had turned too far and we were all on an inevitable path of implosion.

The Child Protective Services people eventually left with the police, and Dad went into the bathroom to take several deep, long drags on his crack pipe.

Several days later I was downstairs with the other kids while Dad and Ginny were upstairs in their room, as they usually were. We were all surprised when, BAM, Tawny and Pastor Jeremiah walked through our door with Bibles in hand. Tawny had also brought her daughter, Nikki, with her and I couldn't remember the last time I'd seen any of them. We hadn't been going to church recently, and Tawny and Nikki had left our family a long time ago. Now they were here like crusaders of God, as Tawny hoped Pastor Jeremiah could perform an exorcism on my dad. I think Tawny thought an exorcism would stop Dad from taking drugs, but I never knew why she chose that particular day to show up. Maybe she and Dad had been seeing each other and I didn't know about it. If that were the case, the hair-pulling fistfight that Tawny and Ginny got into would make more sense. I also didn't realize it then, but Dad and Tawny were still legally married. Their divorce would not be finalized until 2003.

The entire incident scared me to death. Because we hadn't seen Tawny in a long time, her just being in our home was a shock to me. As soon as she arrived Tawny began telling Dad and Ginny where to sit for the exorcism. Barbara and Tucker laughed at this, because they thought it was hysterical that Tawny would try to tell

Dad what to do. I'm not sure what happened next, because I was swept away into a room by one of my siblings and told not to come out until someone came to get me.

After that, Dad probably sensed that officials would be back with legal documents that would force us to be taken away from him. But my dad is a smart man; he turned proactive and beat them to it. First, he purchased tickets for Barbara and Tucker to go to Alaska. Our mother was getting married again, and it was a great reason to send these two children to help her celebrate her big day. Dad then flew to Colorado and spent two weeks in his father's tiny travel trailer getting sober.

To ensure that no one was in residence when Child Protective Services returned, if indeed they did return, I was sent to live for several weeks with Dad's friend (and exorcist) Pastor Jeremiah. Dad has since told me that he doesn't remember my going to stay with the pastor, but I remember it very well because it was here that I first remember no longer wanting to be the "good girl." Until this point in my life I had always been the cooperative daughter, the kid who wanted only to please. But this family was much stricter than I was used to. I also missed my brothers and sister terribly.

Sadly, the incident with Child Protective Services had changed me. After all, I reasoned, what had being a good girl gotten me? A dysfunctional family and no friends. Running away after I had been taken was the first big defiant thing I had ever done, and I now felt a strong need to rebel, to act like my sister and brother— even my dad, for that matter.

One day I went to the grocery store with Pastor Jeremiah's family and I had an urge to act out. Back then cigarettes were not kept inside locked shelves, and I quickly grabbed a pack of Benson & Hedges and hid it in my pant pocket until we got back to the preacher's house. I was so excited to run down the hill near their house and smoke. This was not the first time I had smoked a cigarette—they had been introduced to me at about the same time as the pot smoking.

When I came back up the hill for dinner I was confronted about the smell of tobacco on my clothes, but I lied and said I had not smoked anything. I knew they knew I was lying, but by this time I was convinced these people were total squares. However, I was way cool, and they were just trying to stop me from having fun.

Lying is something every child tries at least once. When I discovered that no one challenged my lies to any extent, it opened a door to a new world. I could now get away with things I would never have dreamed of a few short months ago.

★

By the time I returned from Pastor Jeremiah's to Dad and Ginny, school was out for the summer and he had moved us to another house. Ginny's son, Andy, had not made the move, though. Because Dad was so concerned about the possibility of Child Protective Services taking his children, he and Ginny arranged for her son to live with his dad in California. I had nowhere else to go, so I was the only child living there. Also, I was Baby Lyssa. I was Dad's baby girl and I never went too far from him.

That summer I didn't see much of Dad. He was either busy with his business, or busy with Ginny. I was left to pretty much fend for myself. With no one paying attention to household chores, conditions soon became so bad that there was little food, no clean clothes or dishes, and maggots flourished in the dishwasher. Yes, maggots. Dad was horrified when I pointed them out to him, and he and Ginny made a brief attempt to clean the place up.

I also did what I could to keep our home tidy, but I was still only eight. On the cleaning front I swept up what must have been thousands of maggots from that house. I remember watching them curl themselves up into the dustpan before I threw them out the back door. For meals, one dish Dad liked that I could make was scrambled eggs. I often made them for him and Ginny, but I always seemed to choose a time to cook when Dad was so high that he was uninterested in eating. There was only so much I could do, or in fact, even knew to do.

I did know, however, that life was supposed to be better. I had seen glimpses of this in the way my classmates dressed and acted. I had also overheard snatches of conversations about what life was like for them. Every human has basic survival instincts, and over the next few months mine kicked in big time. Somehow I knew that I had to eat regularly and get enough rest. But the fact that I was left to my own devices, and that it was summer and I had no friends to play with, opened the door to the next step of my descent.

Four

★

Molester or Friend?

*I*t *is a sad* fact that many children fall through the cracks. When it comes to abuse of any kind it is important that parents recognize signs such as lying, stealing, and a sudden drop in grades. I look closely for these signs in my children and guarantee any warning sign will not go unnoticed. I do this through supervision. Unlike my parents did with me, I know at all times where my daughters are, who they are with, and what they are watching or listening to. Close supervision also makes it hard for abusers to find vulnerable children, or for those kids to fall through the cracks.

This is more important now than ever, as kids these days are exposed to far more references to sex and drugs in music and commercials than they were even a decade ago. I do my best to protect my daughters from some of that by limiting what they are exposed to. That's why my ten-year-old daughter is far less comfortable about the idea of sex and drugs than the average girl her age. As an example, now that Abbie is in the fifth grade her school requires her to do her homework in an agenda planner that they hand out to students on the first day of school. On the back page of the planner is an antidrug ad. Abbie was embarrassed just to read the ad and really was shocked that the ad had the word "drug" in it.

On the other hand, Serene (the daughter I gained when I married Bo) at age seven frequently does the booty dance and has even "humped" on my youngest daughter, Madalynn. There have been times when I have had to take Abbie out of the room when Serene acts like that. Because Serene lives with her dad, much of what goes into her head is out of my control. But I do what I can and hope that my influence will have an impact on her. I love that little girl very much. I know now that many of my childhood experiences, however unpleasant, prepared me for other, more challenging experiences. That's why I am very protective of Abbie, Serene, and Mady. In fact, I advocate for them and myself better than the best of mother bears. But when I was a child I did not have the ability to speak on my own behalf. No child does, but due to my life circumstances as a child, maybe I had even less skill in this area than other kids.

When fall rolled around Dad was so afraid that Child Protective Services would take me again that he was afraid to enroll me in school. I guess he thought if CPS didn't know I was still in Hawai'i they wouldn't come looking for me. So instead of classrooms and friends, I spent my entire fourth-grade year home alone. Dad and Ginny were there, but I rarely saw them, as most of the time they stayed in the bedroom. Drugs had taken hold of Dad again, and this time he really lost his way.

Most days I'd wake up on the filthy couch in our living room. Then I'd find a bag of Cheetos somewhere, go back to the living room, and turn on the television. After that I'd pull my blanket (which probably hadn't ever been washed) around me. There I'd sit, just inches away from the television screen, all day. When I got too tired to watch any more I'd fall asleep on the couch. I didn't go to school and I didn't play with friends, as I had none. I really was as lonely and isolated as a child could be.

Technically Ginny was supposed to be homeschooling me, but I don't remember that we had many school sessions. She was too wrapped up in my dad. I don't remember that I was signed up through a homeschool program in the school or a homeschool association, but Ginny and I did go to a store to get some fourth-grade books, and once in a while she gave me a few assignments. I hate to admit it, but when Ginny was busy with Dad I'd read the teacher's copy of the book so when she tested me I did well, even though I didn't study. I tend to think "homeschool" was just a term Dad or Ginny had ready to throw out if anyone ever asked about me.

Every day when I woke up I hoped that this would be the day when Dad would come out of his room and spend some time with me. I missed all the things we used to do together as a family, the parades, fishing, swimming, Bible stories, and all the family time we shared. Barbara and Tucker were in Alaska, and Leland was off on his own. I missed them all so much.

Leland, in fact, was now a dad himself, as his son Dakota had just been born. I was still fascinated with children who were younger than I, babies included, but we didn't see much of Leland during this time. I think he saw what was going on in Dad's life and didn't want any part of it, so he stayed away.

Sometime that fall I became so desperate for my dad's attention that I went to extreme measures to try to find it. One day I spent hours giving myself about a hundred hickeys all over my body. Then I ran to Dad and said, "Dad, look! There's something terribly wrong with me." Dad gave me one dry look and replied, "The only thing wrong with you is that you gave yourself a bunch of hickeys."

Still crying out for attention, one afternoon I actually jumped out of a tree with the full intention of hurting myself. I thought if I were hurt, surely my dad would take some notice of me. I planned the jump in detail. The tree was next to our house, and the branch I jumped from must have been about ten feet up. Scratched, bloody, and bruised, I lay on the ground and screamed for my dad to come help me. Then I screamed some more. But no matter how long or loud I screamed, there was no response. This was definitely not in my plan. Eventually, as dusk fell, I made my way up to Dad's bedroom, only to find the door locked and no answer to my knocks.

★

Beth Smith came to visit us twice during this time. Beth was great at bookkeeping and making sense of a business, so Dad asked her to come, as he needed her skills. The first time Beth came I think she stayed in a hotel for several days. But when Beth came to visit our house she found the living conditions in the home so deplorable that she immediately began cleaning the newest round of maggots out of the kitchen. Her number one goal now became getting Dad off drugs.

I was thrilled that Beth was there. Finally here was someone who would spend time with me. I was always seeking approval from Ginny, but she was always too busy when Dad wasn't around. She paid attention to me when Dad was there, but when he wasn't she yelled at me a lot and had a lot of mood swings that were directed at me.

Beth recently said that I was a total blabbermouth during her stay. And why not? It had been so long since I'd had anyone to talk to that all my pent-up words spilled out to Beth. I told her about Barbara's Goth life and that Tucker had gotten arrested for something. When we went to the grocery store I was so glad to get out of the house that I was on hyperoverload. I showed Beth the way to the store and talked nonstop the entire time we were there.

Beth also told me that she was appalled when, during her visit, she and dad went to a movie. Dad apparently pulled out a crack pipe and began smoking it in the theater. Even worse, he couldn't understand why Beth was upset.

Ginny had thrown a fit when Beth showed up, but the two of them had only one major fight that I recall. It was a real doozy, with all the screeching and name-calling you could imagine. The argument took place either on Thanksgiving or a day or so after, and centered around a turkey that Beth cooked. Ginny apparently didn't like the way the bird was prepared, and the fight was on. At one point Ginny howled at Dad, "Are you going to let her treat me like this?" Dad's response was to throw Beth's suitcase out the door along with a lot of yelling and door-slamming. Beth stayed in a hotel for a few days until she could catch a flight back to Colorado; and when Beth left, I went back to my Cheetos, television, and newly washed blanket.

With Beth gone, Nathan, dad's sensei, was the only other person who ever came to our house. Nathan quickly became my only "friend." He began coming over more and more, and before too long Nathan began taking me to his house, which wasn't too far away.

The house was blue with white trim and was in a secluded area. It was furnished in a sparse oriental style, and the thing I remember most about it was how impeccably clean and orderly it was. I had the dramatic contrast of our home, which, in addition to the maggots, was as littered and filthy as a pigsty.

At his place, Nathan and I played Yahtzee, a dice game I enjoyed. But at that time in my life I would have enjoyed any game as long as another person was playing it with me. Unfortunately, Nathan recognized that. Our Yahtzee games quickly turned into "strip Yahtzee," where I'd have to take off a piece of clothing whenever he scored a point. His behavior then progressed to inappropriate touching. At age nine my breasts were starting to develop, and Nathan used to call me "Big Baby Lyssa." I remember his thick fingers and his heavy older body touching me, grabbing my breasts.

I hated it. I hated him for doing it. The anger I feel toward him today is so huge that it could consume me if I let it. But I kept going back because he was the only person in the world who showed me any attention at all.

Nathan never raped me, but his touches were totally inappropriate. I even spent a number of nights sleeping with Nathan in his bed. The first few times I stayed at his house I was going to summer school three days a week, and my classes were much closer to his house than to ours.

I remember cuddling with Nathan, which in a weird, sick way made me feel safe. Now I can't even stand to think about it without tears coming to my eyes and wanting to vomit. But even though I didn't like what he was doing I was never afraid of Nathan, and I never thought of him as an abuser or a molester. In reality he was a pervert, but he was also my only friend.

Nathan's girlfriend was a beautiful woman I'll call Elissa, who was twenty-five to thirty years younger than he was. I wasn't at all surprised when not too long after my dad met Elissa he began having an affair with her. For some reason I told Nathan this and instead of getting mad about it, he instructed me to watch the next time they were together. He wanted me to report back and give him the details, which I did.

I clearly remember going to Dad's door, peeking in, and then telling Nathan. I felt weird, though, when Nathan asked me to mimic the sounds Elissa made. At some point I must have realized that Nathan's behavior toward me was not right and I told Dad. I wanted my dad to stand up for me; I really wanted him to do something to get Nathan's behavior to stop. But instead, Dad just said that Nathan was a creepy but harmless old man.

Nathan was never punished for his behavior toward me, and I often wonder if he ever found other little girls to be inappropriate with. How many other dads let him touch their daughters? I should have told someone else—anyone—what was going on, but in my isolated existence, there was simply no one else to tell.

★

In the midst of my misery, I did find ways to entertain myself. I have always loved nature, and I spent a lot of time outside, climbing trees. Where we lived, if you walked outside the house wilderness was not too far from our door. There were banana plants and lemon and lime trees. I also found avocado, mango, and orange trees, and ate the fruit from all of them. And like many other kids, I invented imaginary friends to play with.

My hours of watching television had given me a worldview of

politics, current events, government, and other things most kids my age were not concerned with. I designated one tree as my "studio." It was high up in that tree that I regularly hosted an imaginary television show. It was a talk show, similar to morning shows such as *Good Morning America*, or the *Today* show. I even had imaginary guests.

One being who brought me some comfort was our macaw, Paco. A macaw is a kind of parrot that usually has a large black beak and a light patch of facial feathers. Paco was red and gold with white on his face and gold eyes. He was so soft! We had brought Paco to the Big Island with us from Oahu. He was a large parrot who was smart and funny, and he gave me many moments of comic relief.

I loved to hold Paco like a baby and rock him, and he seemed happy to let me do so. He was like one of my dolls come to life. Dad also had a lot of "Paco sticks" placed strategically throughout the house. Paco's wings were clipped so he couldn't fly long distances, and between funny waddles across the floor, he used the sticks to pull himself to new heights in our home.

In the mornings Paco would crow loudly, and he sounded like a real crow. Everyone in the neighborhood could hear him. He also used to bark like a dog. One time, to Dad's dismay, I put Paco on my shoulder and walked around the neighborhood.

Paco was also very picky about whom he spent time with. He'd come to family members but kept his distance from strangers. His preference for me made me feel special at a time when I really needed to feel that way.

Other than my nature walks, imaginary TV show, and Paco, I look back at this period as one of the worst of my life. Actually, I am still somewhat amazed that I got through it. My oldest daughter, Abbie, is now the age I was then, and has been given a protected and somewhat sheltered childhood. It is completely unimaginable to me that she would live through anything like I did.

It may have been only a year or so of Dad's intense drug use, but it felt like forever. I know without question that my dad loved me, but he had gotten so involved in his drug-filled lifestyle that I believe that most of the time he didn't give me more than a passing thought. Since then I have learned that forgetfulness, lack of motivation, irresponsibility, short-term memory loss, and a host of other similar behaviors are typical of drug use and abuse.

Nevertheless, I missed my dad. I missed the "fun" dad who was excited when one of us brought home a new pet. I missed the wonderful dad who tried so hard after Tawny left to make a home for Barbara, Tucker, and me. I missed the great man who helped his ex-wife, my mother, when she was in need. I missed the nice guy who worked so diligently to keep a respectable roof over our heads, who took us fishing, who loved his kids so much that he put us in a parade—and made me feel like a princess. That man was my dad, but drugs had taken over his life. The man who lived in the same house as I did wasn't the man he used to be. I desperately wanted my dad back.

I'd get my wish, but it would take many, many years.

Five

Another Move . . . and Several Others

I moved so much as a child that when I became a parent I vowed to provide as much stability in my daughters' home life as possible. When Abbie was a baby that was very difficult for me to do, but Abbie has been going to the same school now since she was three. She and Mady have the same routine every weekday: school, homework, dinner, bath, read a book. My girls thrive on that routine, along with our fun adventures that usually happen on the weekends.

I make this kind of stability a priority because I remember how difficult it was for me to make new school friends from year to year. Plus, I wanted my girls to have lifelong friendships that only stability can provide. My heart aches for military families and other families that are forced to move frequently because of work commitments. It is always hard for children to be uprooted from familiar places and familiar friends. I know Dad did his best, but even though the moves often brought good things, they were always hard.

One of our moves when I was a child happened when Dad broke up with Ginny. He also stopped using and life got a whole lot better. In particular, I loved our new house, as it was in the town of Captain Cook and just a block from Manini Beach.

Without Ginny to "homeschool" me, I landed back in school. And because I had not gone through the fourth grade I had to be tested for grade placement when I reentered. I passed with flying colors and started fifth grade with other kids my age.

I adored my classes and was thrilled to realize that my love of learning had not deserted me. I was especially glad to ride the bus to and from school. This unstructured time with other kids helped as I dusted off my rusty social skills. My time of isolation was over. I had returned to the school where I went with my Samoan friend, Emma, and the first thing I did was look for her familiar face. I was so sad to realize that she no longer attended classes there. After that I just existed during school and waited for the hours to pass so I could go home and do my own thing.

My brother Tucker had recently been back in Alaska with Barbara and our mother, but had gotten into some trouble. After he was expelled from school there Dad brought him home to us in

Hawai'i. I had missed him and was so glad to have another kid in the house. Life was almost ordinary, or as ordinary as it would ever get for the Chapman family.

The biggest problem we had at that time was money—or lack of it. The years of Dad's heavy drug use had taken a toll on his business. With Dad not paying attention, several of his employees had mismanaged "powers." In bail bonds, you and the company you work for guarantee that you and the bonds office will be responsible for the amount of the bail if the accused person defaults on the bond.

For example, if a person is arrested and then released on $10,000 bond, he or she might not be able to pay that much, so they go to a bonds office and pay 10 to 15 percent of the bail (depending on individual state law). The bonds office gets to keep most of that money as compensation for the service. To make this happen, bonds agents have agreements with local courts. They also have an arrangement with an insurance company, bank, or other credit provider. This eliminates the bondsman having to deposit cash with the court every time a defendant is bailed out.

If the defendant fails to appear in court on the designated day and time, the bonds agent is allowed to bring the defendant in to recover the money paid under the bond, usually through a bounty hunter. In most jurisdictions, bond agents have to be licensed to do business.

In the bail bonds business, we pay the courts with checks that are called "powers," which is short for a power of attorney for that person for the specific alleged offense. At some point Dad realized that seventy-five to a hundred of the powers were missing. Dad was audited, and the state shut him down and took his license. This meant that he could no longer do business as a bail bondsman. Dad was sober but completely broke and up to his neck in debt with the insurance company.

But life wasn't all doom and gloom. With his mind functioning again on a more regular level, Dad took Tucker and me to the beach every day. We had so much fun! Dad began spear fishing again, and Leland began coming around more often. It was so great to see him and baby Dakota. Plus there was a spark in my dad that I hadn't seen in a long, long time. Life was good and I was happy.

We had also gotten a dog for Tucker and a cat for me. If you are not a pet lover you might think this was a financial extravagance, and in a way it was. But on the other hand those pets provided us with so much love that they were well worth whatever we had to do to keep them happy and healthy—and we did.

With little money to buy food, I began eating dry cat food as if it were cereal. I remember one day about this time Dad cashed in all his change and got about fifty dollars. I told Nathan about it, because I thought it was so much fun changing all the money. But Dad got really mad at me. I was too young to understand my dad didn't want others to know about his financial troubles, and I remember him trying to cover up both the story and my confusion.

Dad was so sad the day he took us to the welfare office to get food stamps so we could eat. There was a look on his face that I hope never to see again. No matter what, until this point he had always been able to provide for us. I am sure that it broke his heart to take charity, but we had to have food.

One day after school I grabbed some change from a drawer at home and went to buy a Welch's strawberry soda. This was something I did every day, so I didn't think I had done anything wrong. But on this day when I came back with my drink, Dad was furious because I apparently had just spent all the money he had saved.

I knew we didn't have a lot of cash, but I didn't realize we were that bad off. The fact that the only money Dad had was a bit of change in a drawer unsettled me. I wasn't prepared, however, for the news that greeted me when I came home from school one Friday afternoon shortly after that. Dad told Tucker and me that we were moving back to Colorado that coming Sunday, just two days away.

We spent the next day and a half packing up what little we had. Although we had moved many times, I was devastated that we were moving again. I loved my school and new friends. I loved going to Manini Beach, and honestly, I barely remembered Colorado. This move would bring me back to a home I didn't even know.

On the other hand, I was so relieved that I wouldn't be going to Nathan's house anymore that I felt as if a huge weight had been lifted from me. As Dad stopped using drugs and broke up with Ginny, Nathan's presence in our lives had became less and less, although I still saw him far too often for my liking.

I also cried huge crocodile tears when we had to give our dog, cat, and Paco away. They were family. Dad told us that we'd be back for them soon, but it turned out that it was many years before I again set foot on Hawai'ian soil, and I never saw those particular pets again.

★

I don't remember the actual plane trip across the ocean, but I do recall the culture shock that I felt when we first drove through Denver. The buildings were so tall and there were so many cars driving way too fast on the highway. The past few years we had lived in a more rural section of Hawai'i, and big-city life was new to me. Now I smile to myself when I think of this, but I was also shocked to see that so many white people lived in Colorado. I had gotten used to seeing the friendly brown faces of islanders, and looking at people with white skin like me was very odd.

Once we got to Colorado, Dad, Tucker, and I moved into one room in a Motel 6 near Denver. Barbara was living with our mother, and frankly, she and Tucker were back and forth between Alaska, Hawai'i, and Colorado so often that it is hard to remember who was where at any particular time.

Dad then went to work for his older sister, our aunt Jolene. I thought Aunt Jolene was super square, and in reality she was the total opposite of my dad. She never swore and was appalled by my dad and his ways. Her husband worked for the federal government, and all in all, they were a very conservative couple.

Aunt Jolene was also in the bail bonds business, and Dad had no trouble performing his duties for her company. Because he and Jolene were so very different, however, they had a contentious relationship. This was probably something that started when they were kids and decades later had gotten only worse.

She was kind enough, however, that when Dad caught jumps (people who had jumped bail) for her she sometimes babysat me. Jolene lived on Denver's "Bail Bonds Row," a quirky street of old homes near the courthouse that have been converted into bail bonds offices. Jolene and her family lived on the top floor of one of the houses and did business on the ground floor.

I remember that Aunt Jolene had a son around my age. I was a little jealous of my cousin, because he had every toy you could imagine and the loving parents I always wanted. He and I did not get along, so the two of us carried the familial dislike of each other from one generation to the next. I am not sure why he didn't like me, but I didn't like him because he never let me play with his toys or games. Instead, I had to sit on the floor and watch him play.

I also thought that Aunt Jolene acted like she was helping us out of pity. At the time I didn't understand how we went from one extreme kind of lifestyle to the other. When we lived on Puuwai Alii in Kailua Kona with Ginny we had a pool, a dumbwaiter, and we each had our own bedrooms. Now we were all crammed into one room at a Motel 6. The only thing exciting about our living situation was that there was a pool. But the pool was covered for the winter, and I remember staring day after day at that pool cover, wishing it was time for it to come off.

My aunt paid for our room at the Motel 6. I remember that the cost was $39.99 a day, because it was posted on a card on the inside of the door. That, among other monetary things, was a source of much argument between Dad and his sister, and I remember trying to stay out of the way as they had one fight after the other. Standard bounty hunter fees are 10 percent of the bail amount. If Jolene needed Dad to catch a $10,000 bond who skipped, then Dad's pay should have been close to $1,000.

I think Aunt Jolene felt that if she paid for the room, watched me, and gave Dad a little money for gasoline and incidentals, that was all she needed to pay. There may have been other factors I was not aware of, though. I am assuming that she paid our airfare from Hawai'i. She may even have paid off some of Dad's debt, so what she didn't pay to Dad may have been going to repay his debt to her. But what irked me was the air of superiority that she lorded over us.

This may be why Dad began taking me on some of his bounty hunts rather than have his sister watch me. Although Dad has told me that he first began taking me on bounty hunts when I was about two, my first memories of this happened in Colorado when Dad had no one to watch me. I was very curious about the fugitives Dad captured, and I remember asking them things such as "Why are you bad?" and "What did you do?" I also remember that after one catch I accidentally got one of my suckers stuck in a fugitive's hair—he was in the front seat with Dad and I was in the back. I can just imagine what the guy thought!

Dad always instructed the "bad guys" to be polite to his children, and for the most part, they were. Just as it was shown on the show *Dog the Bounty Hunter,* Dad always talked to the fugitives he caught and tried to encourage them along a better path. "Find them and fix them" has always been his motto. Not all bounty hunters are like this, but Dad has such a good heart that he always wants to help someone if he can—and if it's in their best interest that he do so.

I can attest that while you hunt a person you become infatuated with them. You learn about their families, habits, and hobbies, and when you finally meet them and the cuffs are on you almost want to hug them in relief and sympathy.

When I wasn't on a bounty with Dad, I hoped he would remember to buy something for dinner. He often worked long hours, and when I wasn't with him he couldn't always get away to see that Tucker and I were fed. I knew Dad was trying to dig himself out of a huge financial hole; essentially we were starting over. Because of that I was glad that he was working so much, but it made our mealtimes very irregular.

After a number of weeks or months, Dad had enough of the fights with his sister. That's why Dad jumped at the chance when Beth Smith (now Barmore, as she had married—and divorced— Dad's friend Keith Barmore) asked Dad to house-sit and watch her daughter, Cecily, while she was away for a few days. We packed up our things and moved to Beth's house, which was nearby. I had bumped into Beth a few weeks earlier in the back alley of Aunt Jolene's shop. Beth worked for another bonds company on Bail Bonds Row and gave me a toy, a magnetic drawing board. Beth was very nice to me and I remembered her stay on the Big Island and how much she didn't like Ginny. That alone made her good enough for me.

While I remembered Beth, this was the first time I had met Cecily, who was three or four at the time. I thought Cecily was by far the cutest little girl I had ever seen. I wasn't the only one who thought she was adorable, though, as Cecily had just won the Little Miss Colorado pageant.

Beth's house was a nice three- or four-bedroom home with a basement and a huge yard. The house was full of toys and food, and compared to the Motel 6 I felt like we were living in a castle.

The few days quickly turned into a much longer stay. One reason was that Tucker and I had not been enrolled in school in Colorado, even though the weeks or months we spent at the Motel 6 were during the school year. Beth lived in Green Mountain, which is a nice Denver suburb about twelve miles from downtown. They had great schools and Beth convinced Dad that we needed to be enrolled there.

Shortly after we settled in with Beth, Barbara got into a spat with our mother and was sent back to Dad. I was so glad to see her, but I was soon to find that when she came back our nice new life would change dramatically. Tucker had his partner in crime back, and he began to go off track again. Then Barbara tried to slit her wrists over a boyfriend. She had not wanted to leave Alaska, and the boy she had been seeing was the reason.

I remember being downstairs and hearing Beth and Dad screaming as they held Barbara down to get the knife out of her hands, but not before she had cut herself multiple times. My sister wore long sleeves for a month or so after that.

I am still a little amazed that Beth allowed a man with a drug problem and three troubled kids into her home. She must have been quite overwhelmed! Despite Dad's continual womanizing, Barbara, Tucker, and I had no doubt that Dad loved us more than any girlfriend, but I got the feeling that that idea did not sit too well with Beth. I believe that back then she might have been insecure about the relationship Dad shared with us. For example, Dad always wanted us to go to movies or out to dinner with him, but Beth preferred to have one of her girlfriends watch us when they went out. As far back as I can remember, other than getting high or working, Dad never went anywhere without us—until Beth.

I'm not sure how it began, but at about this time someone started supplying Dad with drugs again. He was not using as often as before, but after the drug use started Dad and Beth began fighting—something that still happens every day. The two of them screamed loudly at each other, and Dad was at times violent toward Beth. I remember him calling her a slurry of names, everything from A to Z. The fights were horrific and showed Dad in a light

I had never seen. He and Beth even broke a number of household objects as they argued for what seemed like hours.

In one instance we were packing our stuff to move back into a motel when Beth angrily tried to open a screen door, but instead smashed her hand through the glass part of the door. There was blood everywhere, and rather than going to a motel, Dad went with Beth to a hospital. Beth still has the scar from that fiasco.

At other times Dad and Beth fought over pills. Specifically, they'd fight over the fact that Beth would not let Dad have any. One time he threw something out of their bedroom and into the hall. In the process the light cover in the hall shattered. I poked my head out of my room to see what was going on, saw hundreds of shards of glass on the floor, and retreated into my room.

It must have been hard on Cecily to see her mom fighting like this. She was barely more than a toddler and had gone, overnight, from being the only child in the home to having three siblings. She and I often played house, and I remember teaching her how to spell her name. No matter how bad things were, I always loved Cecily. However, I did become jealous of the attention Beth gave her, and that made me confused, even though I understood that Beth was Cecily's "real" mom and we were the "step" children. There was a lot of jealousy going on and a lot of egos to massage in that house.

The many crowns, trophies, and sashes in Cecily's room fascinated me. She had won them all in beauty pageants and I soon began competing, too. I especially loved that when I was onstage Beth sometimes called me beautiful, and several times she even cried. To me, her tears meant love and acceptance, and I needed lots of both. I was so surprised when I won first runner- up in the state competition, which put me in line to go to the nationals.

I know a lot of people do not approve of pageants for little girls. JonBenét Ramsey, the little girl whose murder, to date, has not been solved, was on the circuit with us during this time and was in Cecily's age group. Cecily even placed above her a few times. But pageants gave me a hefty dose of validation. I loved practicing my dance for the talent portion, and the attention Beth showered on me when I was getting ready was wonderful. I am very happy that I had the opportunity to compete, even if it was just for a short time.

★

Between pageants, Beth was constantly on Dad about his drug use. And rightly so. While he wasn't using as much or as often as he had been in Hawai'i, any amount was too much. Plus, Ginny called regularly from Hawai'i, and Dad and Beth fought a lot about that. After one fight, Dad told us to pack up, and we moved back to the Motel 6. There were so many back-and-forth moves that I lost count. We might stay a few days or a few weeks at the Motel 6 (or we might stay with Dad's "woman of the week"), and then Barbara, Tucker, and I would move back to Beth's for a day or a month. I don't know how many times we packed up to move, but it was enough that I began to keep all of my things stuffed under my bed in a large plastic trash bag. It was simpler that way. When we heard the words "Kids, pack your shit," all we had to do was reach under the bed and head for the car.

All of these moves were hard on us, but it also must have been hard on Beth and Cecily. It is a testament to Beth's deep love for my dad that she put up with as much as she did. Anyone who has been around a person who uses drugs knows how much the missed appointments, forgotten errands, and general irresponsibility trickle down to everyone involved with the drug user. Dad's drug use kept all of us off balance.

Another problem for me was that Beth and I never really clicked. All of the other women in Dad's life had absolutely adored me. But not Beth. It might have been that I wasn't as young and cute as I was when the other women had been around. It could have been that I was in a transitional phase from good girl to someone who lied on occasion and didn't care all that much about anything. Or, most likely, the reason Beth and I never clicked is that we are just two very different people. That happens even in the best of families.

At the time I also felt that Beth picked on me. For example, I had never used a curling iron, and she regularly commented to me after I tried to use one that my hair looked funny. One time we both struggled with the iron and my hair, and the end result was that I had a huge burn on my neck from the curling iron. I think now that picking on me was Beth's way of trying to help me. After all, I was the little girl with the dirty clothes, unwashed hair, and ragged fingernails. I probably needed a lot of help. But I didn't understand her way of trying to assist me, and animosity built.

Resentment also reared its head when we were living with Beth and Cecily. I'm not sure if Dad saw it, but suddenly there were a lot of people competing for his attention. I didn't understand what it was initially, but over time I realized that tension in Beth's home increased every time Dad paid special attention to me or to Barbara or Tucker.

I am sure that Tucker and Barbara's acting out was terribly hard on Beth, too, especially as I was the only one of the three of us who even halfway listened to her. That might be why I took the brunt of her frustration and discipline, only to be overcompensated with kindness when Dad was around. It was one more thing in my life to be confused about.

I now know that a child learns what he or she is taught, and I was being taught that men disrespect women, hit them, and scream at them. I also learned that what couples do is fight and scream for hours, then everything can go back to normal. At the drop of a hat the same two people who were just at war, now are a happy couple.

I had also learned to keep secrets. It was an unspoken rule in our family that we were never to speak about what we saw or heard at home. We had learned that lesson in Hawai'i, but it continued here.

At school I was still in the fifth grade, but I was no longer the only troubled kid in my class, as I had been when I went to school in Hawai'i. Now a few other kids my age were smoking and in relationships with older boys. I had finally found friends I could relate to.

I started stealing liquor from the house and pot from my brother and sister. I rebelled, and did not care about anything other than boys, alcohol, and drugs. At home, my brother and sister took great joy in teasing me in cruel ways. I remember Tucker hanging me by my hair out a window. In addition to being totally frightening, it hurt more than you could imagine. I also remember being put in the dryer while Tucker turned it on and held the door shut from the outside. To this day I don't feel comfortable in small, dark places. When I told Dad or Beth what they were doing to me my siblings would be punished, and before long I was just the family tattletale. During this period I got drunk for the first time. I remember thinking how all my problems went away when I was drunk. Like pot, booze provided me another escape from the crappy life I was stuck in. Role models are so important. I wish I'd had a mentor who could have shown me that drugs and alcohol were not the way, that I had other choices. But it was not to be.

I desperately wanted control of something in my life, including the ability to make my own decisions. But most of all, I wanted out from under Beth and Dad's control. I would get my wish very soon, but sometimes wishes aren't all that they seem.

Six

★

The Quiet Haven of Alaska

*M*_{otherhood is by far} the greatest joy of my life. I love seeing the day-to-day growth of my daughters, and I revel in their creative efforts and progress. This progress comes in many shapes and sizes. For example, Abbie recently came to me and asked the difference between Democrats and Republicans. I believe that being a mother sometimes means not forcing my own beliefs on my child. Instead, I want to let her make her own decisions.

Of course, "What are you, Mom?" was one of her first questions. So I explained the main differences between the two political parties without prejudice and added that the decision was one she would not have to make until she was much older and could vote.

Madalynn's progress is on a much less intense level. I enjoy seeing her amaze people with her extensive vocabulary and her ability to hold a conversation far beyond her years. She has always picked up on things quickly and was walking at nine months. She also was potty trained by one year and swimming on her own by age two. Mady amazes me every day with her ability to complete so many tasks effortlessly.

Not all parents get to experience this gift, and at certain times in my life either my mother or dad was absent for long periods. When I did reconnect, it was always a little different from what I thought or hoped it would be.

When I was ten I went for a visit during spring break to see my mother. I'm not sure why Dad decided this would be a good time for me to go. Maybe he thought that since I was growing up I needed my biological mother more. Or maybe he and Beth just wanted some time alone. By then my mother was living in Healy, Alaska. Healy is a small town of about a thousand people in the center of the state with a beautiful view of the mountains. This was the first time I had seen my mother since the brief time she lived across the street from us in Hawai'i, when Nicholas was born. I also hadn't heard from her at all during those years—not one birthday card, Christmas card, or phone call, other than the occasional screaming match between her and Dad on the phone. Once in a while Dad would make up a card for me and tell me it was from my mother, but I recognized his handwriting and called him out on it every time. I love that he tried, though.

I was excited and a little apprehensive about spending time with my mother. On one hand, I would have done anything to get out of my chaotic living situation in Colorado. All the moving and fighting left me feeling very nervous, and it was nowhere near the positive environment that a child needed to be in. I was hoping to find a few days of peace and stability with my mother.

On the other hand, I was flying into an unknown. I was just at the age where I was beginning to wonder why my mother had left me all those years ago. Why hadn't she come to see me? Why didn't she call? I realize now that she must have been getting reports about me from Barbara and Tucker. Maybe my mother thought that because I was so young it would be easier for me if she didn't have any contact. I also didn't yet understand that distance and financial constraints played a part, although I would much later realize that there were other factors as well.

Even though I was ten, I was also still puzzled about the role of "mother." Maybe my mother was doing what mothers are supposed do. Thinking back, I hadn't ever been in one place long enough, or had any close friends for a long enough time, to gauge the actions of the mothers of my friends. Did they stick around? Was there just one mother, like we had just one dad? All I had to go on was Tawny, Ginny, Beth, the herd of nannies, and the many other women who had been in and out of our home. It was all so perplexing, but long story short, at that time in my life I would have given anything to get away from Dad and Beth—even for a while. I was beyond thrilled that I was on a plane to Alaska.

For some reason, Barbara and Tucker were already in Alaska,

so I flew north by myself. I was also on an earlier flight than originally planned, so when I landed in Fairbanks late one morning, I had to wait for my mother to show up. It seemed like the longest wait of my life, but the airline staff was great and even let me play with some computer software that moved the Jetway back and forth.

Eventually, though, I became bored—and anxious. What would my mother look like? Be like? When I finally saw her curly hair and bright smile, she enveloped me in a huge hug. Right away I could see that she was light, free, and playful. I really hoped that during this visit I would not have to experience the exhausted feeling I got at Dad's after yet another family fight. And I didn't. My mother was bubbling with happiness—and bordering on silliness. I was too naive to make the connection between the empty bottle of booze in the backseat of the car and her happy mood. Thank goodness a friend of hers was driving.

I knew that by this time my mother had gotten married to a man named Mark Bargas. Mark often worked in a small town in the northern part of the state, so I didn't see him very much on that trip. My younger brother Nick had by now grown into a little boy and was about four years of age. Younger kids still fascinated me, and while Nick was the perfect age for me to play with, I don't remember that I spent all that much time with him.

Despite my apprehension, I really did love my time in Alaska. Even though I wanted to feel a lot closer to my mother than I did, I thought it was cool that she let me drink coffee. I loved the ritual of adding cream and sugar and felt very like an adult when I took a sip. I especially enjoyed it because coffee was a privilege I wasn't allowed when I lived with Dad or Beth. Coffee was a big deal for me because I was in such a hurry to grow up. I've never quite understood why that was, unless I just wanted to get out on my own and away from the daily disorder of my life.

Coffee sticks in my mind because it is a good example of one of the main differences between Dad's house and my mother's. In Alaska there were few rules and life was unstructured. That wasn't necessarily a good thing, but I grasped at every bit of freedom I had there. My mother allowed us to go out with our friends, and we walked all over that town. It was my chance to be social, to be free to make my own choices—which was usually to smoke pot and flirt with boys.

The second reason why I loved this little vacation was that the household was quiet. Once I had some distance and perspective, I realized that Dad and Beth didn't just fight regularly then; they fought all the time. About everything. I know now that Beth was trying hard to get Dad off what drugs he was still using and that he kept sliding back into that lifestyle. But when I was ten, that wasn't so clear to me. All I knew was that most of the words spoken when we lived with Beth were loud and angry.

Finally, I realized that my mother was a fun person to be around. She was always the life of the party, and could find a reason to celebrate at the drop of a hat.

That visit I got a welcome and smiling face from my mother, and it was everything I needed. Because they were older, Barbara and Tucker had always bounced back and forth between our parents, and since Barbara had hit puberty she had spent most of the time with our mother. Dad once told me that he felt a girl needed her mom when she reached that age.

I had hoped to spend a lot of time with my siblings during our stay, but that was not to be. Barbara and Tucker had convinced our mother that they were old enough not to need a curfew or follow any rules she may have set for them. Barbara was fifteen then and Tucker about fourteen, far too young to be so free. But Mark and my mother thought it was okay. Consequently, my older siblings were rarely home.

One day when both Barbara and Tucker *were* home, Tucker asked me if I had ever been whitewashed. I didn't know what that was, but Tucker said, "Come on. I'll show you." We then went outside into the deep spring Alaska slush and he dunked me into an icy puddle that must have been several feet deep. "Whitewashing," I found out, was a sort of rite of initiation to life in Alaska.

My clothes were soaked through and by the time I got back inside the trailer where my mother lived, I was shaking with cold. I stripped off all my clothes and jumped into a shower that was hot enough that my feet burned with what felt like hot daggers. I had not yet learned that when your extremities are frozen to the bone, lukewarm water is the best way to warm up.

Another time, our mother had given Nick and me a few dollars to get some groceries and buy a treat at the corner store. We called it the corner store, but in actuality we got there by walking more than a mile down a wooded trail. On the way back I had my hands full of bags and was also keeping an eye on my little brother. I remember that one of the bags I carried was especially heavy so I must have had a gallon of milk or some orange juice in there.

The trouble began when we were about halfway home. On my right, just off the trail, I noticed a huge moose. Then I looked to my left and saw a baby moose. I made the connection instantly. In addition to undergoing the ritual of the whitewash, I had been warned about the many peculiarities of Alaska life. One thing I learned was that the first rule of Alaska was "Never eat yellow snow." It took me awhile to figure out what that meant. Another warning was never to get between a mama moose and her baby. Moose typically will not attack a human unless they are threatened, but there is nothing more threatening to any species than the possibility of harm to a mama's baby.

If you've never stood next to a moose, I'm here to tell you that they are enormous. I am five-foot-nothing in adulthood, and was much smaller when I was ten, so you can imagine my fear. The second I realized we were in danger I dropped all of the bags, grabbed Nick's hand, and ran as fast as I could back to the trailer. The new shoes that Dad had just bought me became ruined in our race through the slush and muck, and after we dashed into the trailer it seemed like hours before my heart stopped trying to jump out of my body.

I was very sad on the day I got on the plane to go back to

Colorado. I really wanted to stay in this peaceful place with my mother and younger brother. When I walked off the plane and into my dad's waiting arms, the result of my last adventure in Alaska became very apparent. I had cut my hair. Well, apparently I also shaved part of the back of my head in an attempt to look cool. I remember how disappointed Dad was about my haircut. Besides the fact that it probably looked awful, even though Dad now lived in Colorado he was still big on Hawai'ian tradition. One of those traditions was that a woman should not cut her hair until her father passed away. Since moving to Hawai'i I had had my hair trimmed to keep it healthy, but never cut. To Dad, my haircut was a huge sign of disrespect toward him. I don't recall that disrespect was my intent. I'm pretty sure that all I wanted was to look cool.

★

One day shortly after I returned to Dad, he and Beth got into another huge fight. It was around Mother's Day, and Dad had bought a small, corded appliance for Beth as a gift. It appeared that was the wrong thing to do, and Dad once again moved us out of Beth's home.

This time, however, instead of the Motel 6 we moved into the apartment of a woman Dad knew who had twin girls with long hair that they often wore braided. I liked it there until the day I happened to look in the trunk of the lady's car when it was open. It was loaded to the brim with machine guns and lots of packages of white powder strapped with tape, just like I'd seen on television when I was watching a police show. Seeing those things scared me to death and I was very relieved when, soon after that, we left her place for good.

We also stayed several times with a woman I'll call Aurelia. Aurelia was very wealthy and was in the middle of a divorce, but had a huge piece of property in a rural part of Colorado. She had cows and horses, dirt bikes, a motor home, and a lot of other fun things on her farm. She also had several sons of varying ages.

We stayed at Aurelia's for only a short time, and the last morning we were there we woke up to find that one of the cows had died. I've mentioned how much we all love animals, and waking up to a dead cow did not sit well with any of us. We cried to Dad about the poor, dead cow and he promptly told Aurelia that it wasn't going to work out. He then took us back to the Motel 6. That was one time I wasn't sad to go back to motel life.

Between times we were still in and out of Beth's house. I am not sure what Cecily thought about all our coming and going, and I have to give credit to Beth for hanging in there. Without her continual firm reminders, Dad might still be on the path of a drug user.

Beth also provided me one of my main sources of enjoyment: pageants. I was still competing when we were around long enough for me to do so, and the process of dressing up, looking pretty, and performing a talent had become my favorite thing to do. Between pageants and moves I watched as much television as I could, and

I read a ton of books. At school I belonged to a reading club, and I far exceeded the required number of books we were supposed to read. For my efforts, I received a special award. I still smile when I think of that. Some of my favorite books of that time are ones I hope my own daughters will read someday. These include the Judy Blume books, the Little House on the Prairie books, and my favorite, *The Lion, the Witch, and the Wardrobe,* by C. S. Lewis.

★

Eventually the anxiety and depression that resulted from my highly dysfunctional surroundings began to consume me. I so desperately wanted to fit in at school, but all the kids who could have been considered good influences on me had grown far away in emotions and interests. The gap between their home life and mine was just too great.

The only other sets of kids around were the druggies, the juvenile delinquents, and the general troublemakers. No child wants an isolated existence, and I had certainly had my share of that, so I fell, rather hard, into a group of kids in my school whom most people would consider the dregs of society.

To be sure I fit in, I began bringing pot to school. I had started smoking it more regularly, and found it a beautiful escape. I spent a lot of time imagining a better existence—a better, more stable life—and the pot helped facilitate that for me. If I had known how easily pot would serve as a gateway drug for me, how it would take away any motivation I might have had to accomplish anything, I might not have started using it. Or maybe I still would have. My perception of my life was that bad.

Smoking pot was also a way for me to feel that I was growing up. After all, most adults I had come into contact with, the exception being my teachers, smoked it. I thought it was just something that grown-ups did.

Now I can see that I was a true product of my environment. Kids mirror the adults around them, and that is exactly what I was doing. A plumber's kid will play with wrenches and pipe, a doctor's child will most likely have a toy stethoscope, and a pot smoker's child will sooner or later pick up a joint. That's why, while I knew it was wrong, I didn't view the use of pot as a particularly bad thing.

I also found that in my peer group, having a stash of pot made me cool. That was exactly what I wanted. I wanted coolness, to be part of a community of friends, to be the popular girl in my group. But as I mentioned, pot can be a lead-in to a host of other inappropriate behaviors, especially for kids. Cigarettes and alcohol were just two of the other evils I began doing regularly.

At home I became mouthier and stopped all pretense of being cooperative. I watched the negative behaviors of my older brother and sister and imitated them. And at night when I went to bed, the dolls I used to so lovingly cuddle had become just a distant memory.

Seven

★

Actions and Consequences

*L**ooking back over these* years I wish I realized that I had a choice. In ten short years, life had worn me down and I had become apathetic. With no role models to demonstrate a positive direction to me, with no one to encourage me to do well in school, I stopped caring. I should have found someone—a teacher, a counselor, anyone—who would take me under his or her wing. But I didn't.

My role models today do not include one specific person. Instead, they encompass an entire list of people who have influenced me either positively or negatively. For example, I watched the circus that followed the misfortunes of young female celebrities such as Britney Spears, Lindsay Lohan, and Paris Hilton. Sitting back I thought, *Wow, with all the young girls who watch you constantly you choose to drink too much at parties, wreck cars, and do drugs? Why in the world would you set such a bad example with all those young eyes on you?*

If I ever have the power to influence the youth of America, or the world for that matter, I will follow a much more conventional path. I may not have been the best candidate to be a parent or a celebrity, but I know that every example I set had better be a good one. Not only are my daughters watching, but having the eyes of America's youth on me is very humbling.

When I was ten, it never even occured to me that people who could serve as positive role models might exist. I didn't know any counselors, we no longer attended church regularly, and my school attendance was spotty at best. Any adult who might have helped a troubled child like me was too far out of reach. I do realize that kids like me, kids who have troubled home lives, are often the least rewarding to spend time with and to teach. But these kids need positive role models the most. If you are an educator, a coach, a pastor, or a counselor, I encourage you to reach out to kids like me because I know what a huge difference you can make.

With the advent of the Internet, good choices for kids are easier to find today than when I was growing up. Even if there is no computer or Internet access at home, most schools and public libraries allow students to get online. I hope kids who need encouragement from outside their home make the effort to find a good youth center, church, or other program that will show them the many wonderful options there are in life, and also help them get there.

With no role models in sight and with my life continuing to spiral downward, I went back to Alaska to stay with my mother for the summer. By this time I had just turned twelve. I remembered my brief stay more than a year previously and hoped for continued peace and love from my mother.

But this longer stay was not to be the one I envisioned. First of all, my mother had moved from Healy to Anderson, an even smaller town about an hour north. When I was there, Anderson had five hundred residents, six roads, and just sixty-one kids in their one school, which ran from kindergarten all the way through high school. Anderson wasn't even settled until the 1950s, and most of the families who lived there were connected to Clear Air Force Station, which was just five miles south. While Anderson doesn't have the beautiful setting that Healy has, Anderson does have a great view of Denali (a.k.a. Mount McKinley), the tallest mountain peak in North America.

Nick; Tucker; Barbara; my mother; her husband, Mark; and I lived in a trailer in town. When our mother married Mark he had a good job in Anaktuvuk Pass, a small northern Alaska town named after the Anaktuvuk River. Anaktuvuk, by the way, is the English version of a word that means "place of caribou droppings" in the language of the Inupiat, one group of Alaska's indigenous people.

The county the town was in did not allow the sale of liquor, so Mark had a nice little side business going where he'd buy bottles of whiskey in or near Anderson and then sell them for $100 or more in Anaktuvuk Pass. He also sold a little weed up there. Eventually the practice got Mark fired, and by the time I came, he was just hanging out. He was a good cook, though, and I still remember the wonderful "Mickey Mouse" pancakes he used to make for Nick and me.

In the late 1990s, Anderson had little to offer in the way of kid-friendly activities or entertainment, so we made our own fun. For example, Mark used to let us have water fights inside the house. With a hose. He also let us shoot BB guns inside the house. Obviously there was even less structure here than I'd had at Beth's. There was no schedule for chores, homework, or other activities necessary to daily life, so I had too much time on my hands.

With five hundred mostly adult residents there was no one my age to hang out with so I fell into a crowd of older kids whom Barbara and Tucker already belonged to. These were fifteen- to sixteen-year-olds compared to my twelve, and these older kids were, for the most part, not honor roll students. During this summer I realized that my mother had a problem with alcohol. I had grown up some since I had last been here and by this time had learned firsthand about the effects of overindulging. I now knew that what I had perceived on my first visit as bubbly fun was, in fact, drunkenness. My mother and Mark drank socially, but it often got out of hand. When they were both drunk my mother and Mark began fighting every bit as loudly as Dad and Beth did, just not as often. This was a shock to me because I didn't know that my mother could scream at another person with such intensity. It also brought back the unsettled feeling of anxiety I had when I was with Dad.

After I had been in Anderson a few weeks, and after another rousing fight between the adults in the house, my mother tiptoed into my room with a large bottle of E&J brandy. "Shhhhhh," she whispered as she put the brandy in my closet. "Don't tell Mark that it's here." Mark inevitably found the bottle, and when they moved the fight into the garage I could still hear the ugly name-calling between them through the closed door to my room.

One day Mark told us he had to run an errand. When he didn't come home right away my mother alternated between being really angry and distraught with worry. Mark finally called three days later to tell her he had broken down in Healy and the car had been towed. That's why he couldn't come home. Mark assured her that he was trying to find parts for the car and would be back soon.

I'm not sure whether my mother bought that story, but she acted as if she did—at least until a pawnshop in Fairbanks called her to let her know that Mark had pawned the car. I didn't see Mark at all after that, and a few years ago was saddened to hear that he had passed away in a car accident. He may have been irresponsible, but he sure knew how to let a kid have some fun! Since then I have become close with two of his daughters, who both live in Colorado.

★

My mother was now a single parent. She had not worked when she was married to Mark, as his little side business had paid the bills. My grandma gave us some money to get us through, but now my mother had to find a way to support us. In a town of five hundred people that's not easy to do, as there are not a lot of job opportunities. We did have one big industry in Anderson, however, drinking, and my mother quickly found a job as a bartender at the Dew Drop Inn.

The job was perfect for her because, I have said, my mother liked to drink. She was also bubbly and social, and people loved her. But after Mark left, my mother developed a pattern. She got up late in the morning and started drinking coffee. As the day progressed she'd switch to beer and by evening she was knocking back the hard stuff at work.

I did some babysitting by day so I wasn't home a lot. And because the bar's policy was "as long as there is a customer the bar is open," my mother often didn't get home until the wee hours of the morning. Consequently I never saw her, and that's when I really started being free.

The physical result was that I started wearing belly shirts (short, cropped T-shirts), piercing various parts of my body, and dying black streaks into my hair. I looked halfway between a Goth and a slut. My mother must have felt the need to have some control over me, so she told me to be sure to be home when the streetlights came on. The problem with that was in that part of Alaska in summer, it was light all the time and the streetlights rarely, if ever, were lit.

Actions and Consequences

I had lived through addiction with my dad. Now I was disappointed to find I was going through it again with my mother, although this time it was different. The main reason was because I still didn't realize the seriousness of either drugs or alcohol. I didn't understand why CPS had tried to take us away from Dad because of his use of drugs, but no one cared if my mother drank. Lots of people in my world did drugs and even more drank, so neither was unusual for me although my mother did seem to drink more than her share.

While I was concerned for my mother, I found that I liked the few new kids I had met. While I considered them friends at the time, these really were older kids who just let me hang out with them from time to time. This group of kids held parties every week, and even though our behavior was age-inappropriate, it was one of the few times in my life that I felt I had any companionable friendship.

The first day I was in Anderson I was walking a bike that my mother had found for me. Up the street I met a boy named Bo Bailey. We went over to the park and I told him I wanted to try the slide. "No," he said, "please don't go down the slide. I just peed on it." From then on Bo and I were great friends. We are still friends to this day.

One afternoon after I had been in Anderson for about a month, I went to the home of an older girl whom I'll call Ericka to get drunk. Yes, the family curse of addiction was starting to affect me, although I did not yet know it. All I knew was that pot and alcohol were becoming not only my escape, but also something I looked forward to very much.

I wish someone had been there at that time to pull me back, to show me there were other ways to enjoy life. Maybe if Beth had been there to encourage me in pageant competition, or if a mentor had been handy to steer me into sports, I would not have found chemical enhancements so enticing.

Anyway, I'd had too much to drink and felt an overwhelming need to tell someone about Nathan and his molestation of me. So when I was hanging out in Ericka's bedroom after school, I told her. We had been smoking pot and drinking when the conversation paused, and I took that opportunity to blurt out my secret. She wanted to know who molested me, and in that odd way that is common to many victims, I found I needed to protect my predator. So instead of saying it was Nathan, I told Ericka that my stepfather had done it. Mark was out of the picture anyway, and I didn't think it would go any further. Boy, was I wrong.

The next day I was really hung over when the police began banging on our door. Unbeknownst to me, Ericka had contacted them. I am sure Ericka thought she was protecting me with her call, but it turned into so much more—and this time it really was my fault. While I had hated the molestation, I still didn't realize how very wrong Nathan's behavior had been, so I was shocked that the police were making such a big deal about it.

At first the officers were rude to my mother because they thought she had allowed the abuse to happen there in Anderson.

"Lyssa Rae," she yelled to me in my room, "you tell them Mark did not do this. You tell them the truth, that it wasn't your stepdad but your real dad."

I was sitting on my bed and I have to admit that I was so terrified I couldn't speak. One reason for my fright was that I wasn't sure what was going on; I thought I had done something wrong. I had told a friend something important about me and now the police had barged into our home. I knew I had to go out into the living room and tell the police something—anything—so I did.

"This house is completely safe," I told the officers. "It happened in Hawai'i."

The adults then made the assumption that the molesting had been done by my dad, and to my eternal shame I did nothing to contradict that. If I have one huge regret in life, this is it. I am still not sure why I did not step up and explain about Nathan. The only thing I can think of was that between his "friendship" and his molestation, everything was very confusing. Maybe I so desperately didn't want anything more to do with Nathan that I subconsciously allowed people to believe it was the first man who came to mind, and that was Dad.

Not too long after we had moved back to Colorado, Nathan called me. He started right in with, "How is my Big Baby Lyssa?" and I felt so revolted that I hung up the phone. Just thinking about him made me nauseous, and still does even today. The devastating consequences of my words, or lack of them, began to play out right away. If I had known then the heartbreak it all would bring I would have shouted Nathan's name from the treetops. But I didn't. I didn't understand the seriousness of it. All I wanted was for the police to go away.

My mother immediately filed legal paperwork to keep me in Alaska. I am not sure if my mother really believed me, or if this was another way for her to get a dig in at my dad. Dad had always been good about not saying negative things about my mother, but she did not always reciprocate, especially when she had been drinking. I tend to think that any mother, drunk or sober, would want to believe her daughter about allegations like this.

Dad also used to tell me (and my mother) how much like her I was. I am sure that my mother thought that Dad had some sick sexual fantasy going on with me, when that was the furthest thing from the truth. Dad was never improper toward me, and his physical actions toward me have never been anything other than what was suitable for father and daughter. In short, I think my mother had such strong negative feelings about my dad that she was willing to believe anything I said, or didn't say. I am sure my dad was shocked when he heard what transpired, and I am so deeply sorry that I caused him and the rest of my family pain.

I am also very ashamed to admit that while I hated the molestation as much as I could possibly hate anything, I found that I was beginning to enjoy playing the role of victim. I took pleasure from the attention the situation brought me, and for a little girl who had been through all I had, the attention was a welcome thing.

I was also glad that I was staying in Alaska. It was quieter there, and I had friends. Plus, in Alaska I didn't have to move all the time. Beth was also not constantly on me about my hair being messy or my room not being clean. I know Beth was trying to provide some structure in my life, and while I can look back with gratitude for her efforts now, when I was twelve her expectations just grated on me. There were no expectations—and there was no structure—at my mother's. What twelve-year-old doesn't like that?

★

The months wore on, and in the fall I started school in Anderson. We lived at 345 D Street, which was a little over a mile from the school. Mom didn't have a car then, so every day Barbara and I walked to and from school. It wasn't bad in the fall and spring, but in the winter our damp hair from our morning showers had frozen solid by the time we got to class.

The school itself was nice. All grades K to 12 went there, but there were only four classes: kindergarten to third grade, fourth grade through sixth, seventh and eighth, and ninth to twelfth.

Our principal was also the sports coach, science teacher, and math teacher. The gym had a rock climbing wall, and every student was assigned one of the orange lockers in the center of the building.

Our little family lived in a double-wide trailer, and our mother always made sure we had a good breakfast before we left for school. You might think that with her excessive drinking she would be somewhat disorganized at home, but that was not the case. She always kept a spotlessly clean and cozy house.

The school did not provide lunch, so Barbara and I trekked back to the house, where our mother often made chili cheese hot dogs for us. I loved those so much! Sometimes she'd go to work early and we'd have French fries at the Dew Drop Inn for lunch. If we were lucky, we'd catch a ride from another parent back to school.

I always try to look at every situation from the perspective of other people, and I can see how my mother must have been very stressed during this time of her life. Other than for Nick, she had not been a full-time mother since I was very small, and now she had four children to take care of. In addition, she had an older son from a previous marriage, Jason, who was grown and out on his own.

With the stress of being a single mother of five and having been abandoned by her husband, I think that as much as my mother wanted all of us to live with her, she wasn't prepared for the day-to-day reality of it. Plus she always seemed to be the kind of person who had a hard time fitting in. Now she was a single mom with a ton of kids in a town of mostly married people. It is easy to see why the Dew Drop Inn, and all that lifestyle entailed, became her sanctuary.

★

Even though I tried not to think about it, with every day that passed a custody decision loomed closer. Right after this all began

I started having nightmares about my dad raping me. In my horrible dream we were back in the Motel 6. Before long I was too frightened to even try to sleep.

My mother sent me to a therapist and I was prescribed Trazodone, a tetracyclic used to treat depression and anxiety. This was the first of many drugs I would be prescribed. Eventually they would lead to a pill addiction, but for now my zombielike state made the adults in my life feel like they were doing something positive.

When I told Ericka my secret it never occurred to me that I would have to go to court. And I didn't have the slightest thought that I would have to take the witness stand or that I would have to swear under oath that what I said was true. The hearing was also my big chance to set the record straight. All I had to do was tell everyone that I committed a lie of omission, that it wasn't Dad. Instead, it was someone else. Unfortunately, I didn't do that.

I have had many years to think about my words and actions. I was a messed-up kid for sure. I was doing drugs, was overly sexual, and was considered troubled by every definition of the word. At this time I really didn't care about a thing in this world. I think now that the molestation, the fighting in my dad's home, and the continual moving from place to place had just worn me out. I didn't want to go back to that.

Fortunately, my mother did not want to press criminal charges against Dad. All she wanted was full custody of me. On the appointed day my mother and I appeared in an Alaskan courtroom. Dad was on a speakerphone, and I remember how angry and confused he sounded. I wanted to cry, but my drugged-up state didn't allow an emotion like that to come through.

Over and over Dad said as patiently as he could that he did not molest me and that he had no clue as to why I would say he did. As the trial had gotten closer, Barbara and Tucker had bounced back to Dad, and I felt so sad when they testified against me and for Dad. It had all gotten so terribly out of hand. All I could think was that I just had to get through this day and that no one (other than my dad) would ever know I was living a lie.

My mother was awarded custody, and on our way home from the trial she bought me a milkshake and said, "Thank goodness it's all over and no one was hurt." But that wasn't true. My entire family was hurt by my lack of words, my inability to stand up and tell what really happened.

I have since learned that my actions were typical of a victim of sexual abuse. The desire to protect the molester and the inability to act on your own behalf are integral parts of the deep psychological harm caused by molestation. What I did was a form of unconscious survival. I didn't want to hurt Nathan. I also didn't want to go back to the chaos and constant moving that was life with Dad, so I did nothing and allowed the adults in my life to assume something that was not true.

As you can imagine, my actions caused problems for my family that still exist today. For this I am truly sorry. Picture me on my knees begging for forgiveness with tears in my eyes and you'll get an accurate picture of my sorrow and shame. Whenever my brothers, sisters, and I disagree on something they never hesitate in anger to remind me of what I did. I don't need to be reminded. I live with it every day of my life. But I also take time to remind myself of all the circumstances in my life at the time. If others had been in my shoes, they, too, may have let events unfold around them, as I did. Or maybe not. I believe that God is the only judge, and I have made peace with Him on this.

In our family we have something we call "irrevocable acts." These are serious things that once you do them, they cannot be undone. For example, driving while drunk is a bad thing, but calling the police on a family member who is driving drunk is an irrevocable act because it sets things in motion that can't be stopped. For a Chapman, committing an irrevocable act is cause for scorn, derision, and mistrust, and I had just committed the mother of irrevocable acts.

Eight

★

No Cease-Fire in Sight

The circumstances of my upbringing, although often hard,
taught me the value of a dollar. Today I realize that while
it is sometimes nice to have a designer purse, or a famous label on
my jeans, the quality of my worldly possessions does not make my
character. It is important to me that I instill that concept into my
daughters' minds, for it is a valuable one.

One way I do that is to allow Abbie to earn her spending
money by doing extra things around the house, rather than
just giving the money to her. Abbie also understands that if she
wants something expensive, that I first have to pay rent, buy
food, put gas in the car, and take care of all the other obligations
that are needed for survival. Then we discuss the cost versus the

benefit and oftentimes she decides that the "something" she had once wanted was not so important to her anymore.

Understanding that my self-worth is not tied to money was one of the most significant lessons that living in Alaska taught me. With the trial behind me, I settled into life in Alaska permanently. One thing I loved about living in Anderson was that once a month Nick, my mother, and I made the ninety-mile drive northeast to Fairbanks. With roughly thirty thousand people living there in 1999, Fairbanks was the second-largest city in the state. To me the difference between small-town Anderson and the big city of Fairbanks was like night and day.

The trip was usually the first Saturday or Sunday of the month, after our welfare check came in. The night before we went I'd make sure to get to bed early, as we all had to get up at five-thirty in the morning to make the trip. When we got to Fairbanks we always stopped at a McDonald's. Fast food was one of the things I missed most about living in rural Alaska. After abstaining for a month, McDonald's food tasted so good!

My mother also scheduled doctors' appointments and other errands to fall during our monthly trip. If you have ever lived in a small town, you know how limited goods and services can be. Everything other than our basic weekly shopping had to be done on this one day in Fairbanks.

The last errand on our list every month was a stop at Fred Meyer. Fred Meyer is a supermarket super center similar to Walmart—a store that has everything. We'd spend several hours at Fred Meyer, stocking up on everything we needed for the month, and then we'd make the long drive back to Anderson. It is amazing how much I came to appreciate and look forward to simple things such as shopping and fast food when they weren't part of my daily life.

In June, my birthday rolled around once again. Unlike previous birthdays that were either nearly forgotten or imposed with a ton of family drama, this year I had no expectations about a celebration. We had no money for special gifts (much less a party), and I understood that because every penny was important to us my mother had to work at the bar that day.

That year June 10 fell on a Saturday, a day when my mother usually went into work in the morning to clean the grill and tidy up the bar. I got up late that morning, then wandered out into the kitchen. I was so pleased to find that my mother had left me a loving note and a beautiful pink rose from our garden on our kitchen table. The note read: THE FIRST ROSE OF THE SUMMER BLOOMED ON YOUR BIRTHDAY. COME DOWN TO THE DEW DROP AND I WILL MAKE YOU A MILK SHAKE AND CHEESEBURGER. To this day that birthday stands out in my memory as my absolute best. That simple acknowledgment of my special day made me feel that my mother loved me and was glad I was born. Until then I hadn't been sure that was the case.

Another thing I realized that day was that feeling loved, truly loved, was an unusual sensation for me. I knew my dad loved me and that my brothers and sisters did as well. But love was never acknowledged to me in such a tender manner.

When I was very small, Dad said "I love you" every night when he tucked me into bed. Later, when I was older, when he said the words it was usually before a punishment was handed down. "Because I love you so much I'm going to have to ground you" was heard a lot at our house when I lived with Dad. His way of expressing love and my mother's were both heartfelt, but polar opposites. Since I have grown into adulthood I understand that this is a guy thing. Many men feel uncomfortable expressing their emotions as openly as women do. It doesn't mean they love you less, they just show it differently than women. And besides, there is nothing quite as special as a mother's love.

That's why I felt that this simple, quiet note and the rose from my mother was a beautiful way to express a lovely sentiment. Once in a while life provides us with moments that are extraordinarily special, and that was one of those moments for me. I will never forget the gesture, or the thought behind it.

One final gift came to me that day through my mother: a clear and defined moment when I realized that material things were not important. Love, however, is everything. I carry that thought with me to this day. Even though I now have the financial means to live more extravagantly, I don't, and my home is filled with simple furnishings. Instead of fancy restaurants or expensive clothes I prefer homemade organic dishes and down-to-earth clothing on sale. Instead of a night on the town, I prefer a day at the park with my daughters.

Someday I hope our society will realize what I learned on

my thirteenth birthday, that consumerism is an empty thrill—providing a meaningful moment for a loved one lasts a lifetime.

★

Although my mother worked long hours, money continued to be a trial for us, and that extended to my life at school. While my grades were good and I liked my classes, the other kids eventually noticed that I wore the exact same pair of jeans to school every day, and they weren't always that clean. But that was all I had, one pair of jeans, and they were also the only pants I had. I had gotten them on one of our monthly trips to Fred Meyer and we paid $20 for them, so these jeans that were being mocked by my classmates were a huge extravagance for us.

My breasts were also beginning to develop more, and to my extreme embarrassment, I didn't have a bra. That is something my mother probably noticed, but she came from a type of young women in the 1960s who didn't wear bras. She preferred to go without, so I guess a bra for her daughter was not on her radar. Additionally, because my relationship with my mother was still new, I didn't feel comfortable enough to ask her for one. I wasn't sure how much a bra would cost, but whatever it was, I knew it would be more than we had. I went to school for months wearing my one pair of jeans and trying to cover my breasts with my books.

During this time I also asked my mother if she had a curling iron or a blow-dryer. Of course she didn't. She was a free-flowing hippie chick, and while that was fine for her, those two items would have gone a long way toward making me feel like I fit in. As any teen girl knows, going to school every day with the "wrong" hairstyle opens the door to ridicule and ostracism.

By this time a girls' clique was starting to form in my school. These five or six girls were born in Anderson and had grown up together. There were only five or six major families in Anderson, so most of these girls were also related somehow. A small number of boys also grouped. I wasn't part of any clique. Anderson was so small that new girls just didn't move into the area like I had, so they were slow to accept me. It was bad enough when an individual person laughed and taunted me because I was poor, but when an entire clique did the same, it was too much. I think I went home every day that year in tears.

Today bullying is a hot topic, but not so much back then. I'm not sure if the teachers or other parents at the school noticed what was happening. If not, they should have. Children learn so much socially at that age, and thinking that bullying is an okay thing to do is definitely not okay. That kind of negative behavior and thinking can permeate everything a person does. Before long the bully is only out for himself or herself, and lacks any form of empathy to help or care for others.

I am so glad that this topic is finally getting the attention it deserves, because no one should have to suffer what my fellow students did to me—including my daughter. In Hawai'i, just as it was when I was in school here, my older daughter, Abbie, is one of the only white children in her school. In a recent class discussion on Hawai'ian history, the textbook used the familiar but derogative term for people of Caucasian descent, "hā'ole," and indicated how mean "hā'ole people" were for taking land away from the native Hawai'ian people. The eyes of every child in that class turned to Abbie, and later she was bullied about stealing people's land.

Like me, my daughter had no part in stealing anyone's land. She was nine years old. Fortunately, Abbie told me what was going on and both Beth and I called administrators at Abbie's private school to tell them we found this unacceptable.

While my own mother didn't know about the bullying that was going on with me, she and my therapist did notice that something was going on. Before I knew it my counseling sessions had doubled and I was prescribed more medication.

★

One thing I had learned by the time I was thirteen is that we all have impulsive, and often destructive, behaviors that we turn to in times of stress. For some it might be eating, for others it is alcohol or drugs. What I had seen so far from the women around me was that they defined themselves by the men in their life. From Tawny's pursuit of Dad, to the nannies, to all the other women, the women I knew did not feel complete without a man in their life. This included my mother.

As soon as my mother realized that Mark was not coming back, she began frequenting dating chat sites on the Internet. In Alaska every resident can apply for an annual disbursement of funds called the PFD (Permanent Fund Dividend). These funds range between $600 and $1,500 or thereabouts, depending on the year, and are used to stimulate the economy. A parent is responsible for the spending or saving of their child's PFD, and what isn't spent is supposed to go into an education fund for them.

I had really wanted a computer, and with part of my PFD that year my mother bought a Dell computer and set it up in the living room. While it was "my" computer, my mother was on it until all hours of the night. Dating chat rooms were relatively new at the time, but my mother jumped right into it. I remember hearing the click of computer keys every night as I fell asleep.

Before long, men began showing up at the house. It seemed to me that my mother slept with some of them. I don't think any of them stayed around very long, certainly not long enough for me to remember their names.

One day my mother said we needed a web camera to go with the computer, and with a little more of my PFD we got one. I remember helping her install it, even though I wasn't sure why we needed one. A few weeks later I was looking for a file on the computer and I stumbled across some photos of my mother. But these were not the typical smiling photos of a mom with her arms around her children. These were suggestive photos of my mother in all sorts of poses. In some she was wearing attire that I now know is used in bondage fantasies.

For whatever reason, my mother seemed to need the physical part of a relationship with a man more than the emotional—if you can call a one-night stand a relationship. Once again I was being given a distorted view of the role women play.

★

But all was not terrible during this time. Animal lover that I am, I was thrilled when my mother allowed me to get a beautiful black-and-white cat I named Cinderella. Well, that's what I called the cat until we discovered Cinderella was a boy. After that he was Cinderfella. He had fluffy long hair and was very sweet and affectionate. I have had a lot of cats over the years, and like most of them, Cinderfella was loyal and slept with me every night.

School let out every day at three o'clock, and at three-fifteen basketball practice started. I loved basketball then—and still do. I was number 44 and eventually worked my way up to point guard. Sports were something I was really good at, and in most cases, even though I was tiny, I could hold my own with the boys. I also participated in cross-country and other track events, and I played the flute in the band. I loved when the band got to travel with the basketball team so we could play the national anthem before the games. During this time I was also a straight-A student. I am still amazed that I was able to keep up so well despite all the dysfunction at home.

When my after-school activities were over I came home, shook off any new insults I had received at school, and watched cartoons with Nick and Cinderfella. I especially loved the old *Looney Tunes* cartoons and *Angry Beavers*. Cartoons were a much more appropriate way to escape the stresses of real life, and with Nick and Cinderfella beside me, I could finally relax.

I also spent a lot of time outdoors. I loved four-wheeling and dirt-biking.

Nine

★

Following Mom and Barbara

*T*oday *I wonder why* I was in such a hurry to grow up, and I am careful that my own daughters are allowed to enjoy a normal childhood as long as possible. To make that happen, I don't have cable TV in my house. While we sometimes watch television, we more often pop in a movie or an educational DVD that we view together. I'd much rather go outside and play games such as tag or hide-and-seek with my daughters than plop them down in front of a television anyway.

I also send my older daughter, Abbie, to an all-girls private school. As of this writing, Mady is just two and a half and I have a wonderful nanny whom we all have come to love who cares for Mady and Abbie when I have to work. While I'd rather spend all my time with them, I am a single parent and have work commitments that take up part of my day. I am so grateful, though, to have found this loving, mature woman who values and upholds my standards for my daughters.

I am also totally aware of which songs are on the radio when we are in the car or at home. I fill Abbie's iPod with Christian music and have taught her that there is a big difference between singing about love and singing about sex. My rule is that if she doesn't understand the meaning of the lyrics, then she doesn't need to listen to the song—or sing it. I know every second of every day whom my daughters spend their time with; what they are doing; and what words, music, and other information go into their heads.

Finally, I make sure that I correct any inappropriate tone or words that come out of my daughters' mouths. Children should respect others, especially adults. I understand a child's right to be angry or disappointed, but there are appropriate ways to express those feelings without disrespecting others.

You might think that I am an overly strict and rigid parent, and you would be partially right. I am strict, but having lived through what I have, I know firsthand the dangers out there. Plus I think there is a big difference between being a parent and being a friend. My job is to be a parent. I understand that one day my daughters are not going to like the decisions I make for them, such as saying no to dating, but they know I discipline only out of love. I know if you were to meet my girls you would see two well-adjusted, friendly, active, intelligent, funny, and engaging children who are a delight to be around.

Best of all, I have an open relationship with my daughters, meaning they know they can come to me for anything, about anything, and I will explain or help in a manner suitable for their age. Supporting their individual interests, such as singing and swimming, is important to me and I tell them all the time that I love them with all my heart. They know there is nothing they could ever say or do to change that. Ever.

Because of all of that, I find that every day I become a better parent. And because I am a better parent, every day my girls become better daughters. I do realize that in some ways I am reliving the childhood I never had with my kids, and have become not the parent I wish I had, but the parent I desperately needed. I needed a parent with rules and boundaries mixed with love who could show by example a physically and emotionally healthy way to live. Instead, when I was growing up I was left largely unsupervised, which allowed me to follow my older sister far too closely.

At about the time I entered seventh grade my sister Barbara joined us in Alaska. She had most recently been living with Dad and Beth, but it was time for another bounce, and here she was. While I was thrilled to have my older sister around, it quickly became apparent to me that Barbara liked to party as much as our mother did. She was just sixteen, but boys, late nights, drugs, and alcohol were already the norms for her. And they were beginning to be for me, too. I really loved hearing her stories about boys and parties.

My female role models were definitely modeling a path for

me; it just wasn't a very positive one. I didn't know that yet and I wanted so much to fit in—wanted so desperately to be seen as a cool person—that I began telling friends I had slept with twelve different boys even though I was still very much a virgin.

Like many twelve-year-old girls I was so boy-crazy I could barely stand it. The difference between other girls and me, however, was that I had witnessed far too much while I was still way too young. While other little girls giggled with embarrassment when they thought of kissing a boy, I can never remember a time when I was that innocent.

Instead, when I was twelve I couldn't wait to sleep with a boy, and my mother was the unwitting catalyst that made that happen. One day I walked to the bar to ask my mother something and found her wearing a T-shirt that read SPANK ME and saw that several men were ogling her. Even though I knew she drank, even though I knew she slept with different men, the scene that day shocked me.

I feel sad now when I think of my mother. She really is a very nice and loving person, but alcohol and drugs change us all. The power that the illness of addiction has over so many people, myself included, is heart-wrenching, especially because it affects every member of the family, every friend, every working relationship the addict has. For many years the thing I was most afraid of was ending up like her, always dependent on a man, living the party life, not loving myself, and needing drugs and alcohol to get through each day.

But I didn't realize any of that then. What I saw at the bar that day just gave me more validation that women need a physical relationship with a man to be happy. While I do not advocate unmarried or unprotected sex now, that's why I lost my virginity in the front seat of a car after a party when I was twelve to a boy who was five years older than I. The boy was a former boyfriend of Barbara's, and I remember I was so happy that I finally had sex.

Today even the thought of that night makes me sick. I was far too young to handle the responsibility, and there was nothing loving or sacred about the act. He was a nice boy and a nice friend, but I wasn't in love with him, or he with me. Everything about it was totally wrong.

★

As you have seen, drugs of one form or another had been a given in my life as long as I could remember, but drug use in our family was going to go to an entirely new level. I had been smoking pot on and off (mostly on) since my days in the closet in Hawai'i when I was eight. Barbara and my mother also smoked, but when Barbara returned to Alaska this last time, my mother began giving her pot.

It says a lot that the use of marijuana was so commonplace in our family that a mother would give it to her daughter. In our own version of sibling rivalry, I thought it unfair that Barbara was given pot and I wasn't. When I first asked my mother for some marijuana, she said no, but when I asked several more times, she gave in, and that's how my mother became my supplier. All I can think now is that when you are around anything long enough, it becomes the norm, and for my mother, using drugs and drinking was just part of everyday life.

About the only really normal thing in my life was that I fell in love with the boy next door, or in this case, the boy across the street. Even better, he was in love with me! James Jenkins was a year older than I. He was the star athlete in our school and he was the epitome of tall, dark, and handsome. Before long I was spending every waking moment with James. Our windows faced each other, and I stapled a sheet across mine so he could slip in unnoticed. All we did was hold each other in my bed. And although that, too, was inappropriate for a child of thirteen, I remember feeling so loved and content and secure. James did not know I smoked pot, even though he must have had some inkling of the dysfunction in my family.

To add to that dysfunction, my mother had a new boyfriend, and at about this time he moved in with us. Jimmy Neeley was a really good guy and was a stabilizing factor in my mother's life—and in mine. Back in Colorado, Dad and Beth had just had a baby girl, Bonnie Jo, and all sorts of conflicting emotions were running through my head. *I* was Dad's Baby Lyssa. *I* was his baby girl. The youngest of Dad's children had always been me, and to have a sibling younger than I was . . . well, that was inconceivable to me.

Jimmy's presence also helped us financially. Since Mark had left, we had been dirt poor, and having another income in the household lifted us out of the bottom rungs of poverty. In addition, Jimmy spoiled Nick and me, and I ate up all the attention. I liked him for that, and also because he was someone I felt I could trust. That was important because at some point I realized I was pregnant.

James and my innocent holding of each other had eventually turned into much more. We had tried to be careful, but I was too embarrassed to ask for condoms during my therapy sessions and we had no other access to them. While I knew being pregnant would complicate my life, I had no concept of the seriousness of it all. A month or so earlier Barbara, still just sixteen, had announced that she was pregnant. She had immediately been sent back to Colorado to live with Dad and eventually had an abortion. Two of my friends, including one named Danika, were also in the fifteen-to-sixteen age range, and they, too, were expecting. This, I thought, is what teenage girls do.

Even though I didn't understand the scope of change a baby would bring into my life, I was afraid to tell anyone about the pregnancy. I knew it had to be done, however, so one night I got drunk and told my mother. If I thought she might be supportive, I thought wrong. Instead, she hit me across the face and called me trash. I'll never forget how deeply that word stung. My mother then called James's mom, and more yelling began. Before I knew it Jimmy, my mother, and I were fighting just like Dad and Beth used to fight. Talk about learned behavior!

I was angry with my mother for not supporting me and angry with Jimmy because he took my mother's side. In my anger, I told Jimmy that my mother was dating someone down at the bar. This was a fact my mother had been hiding from Jimmy for some time. Jimmy then stormed down to the bar, and I assume another fight took place.

It wasn't too many days later when Jimmy moved out. I was sad to see him go because I truly liked him. I was also sad because he had moved a huge entertainment center into my room, and now it was leaving with Jimmy. I didn't have to worry too long about that, however, because I was sent back to Denver, this time to live with my grandmother.

★

While I initially resisted the move, it turned out that I loved my time with my grandmother. This was my mother's mother, Grace Katie Worthington. She had raised five children by herself after her husband died and had a no-nonsense way about her. For example, Grandma had a strict five-minute shower rule. There was an actual timer on the shower, and if you weren't done when the shower turned off, too bad.

Grandma also always had supper ready at five o'clock. If you weren't there to eat it, you didn't eat until breakfast the next morning. She was strict, never found the need to swear, and was the most down-to-earth woman that I had ever met. To this day she is one of my main foundations, and I feel so blessed to have her in my life.

In Denver I also was able to reconnect with friends I had made from previous childhood visits. One friend lived up the block, and I went to several parties at her house. It was summertime, so kids were on break from school, which meant that whatever curfews they normally had were relaxed.

I met a lot of people then, but Steve was one who became special. James and I had broken up after the pregnancy news had gotten out and I desperately craved attention. Steve was always around, and that's how he became first a friend, and then a boyfriend. Grandma wisely didn't allow me to have boys in my room, but I lied and told her that Steve was gay. This is yet another thing I am not proud of. My grandma had done nothing but try to keep me on track until the baby was born and I could give him or her up for adoption. That I lied to this kind woman fills me with shame.

Just a few short weeks after I got there, I went to a party at a house that belonged to another friend. I say a party, but it really was a drunken brawl. By the time the friend's parents came home unexpectedly, Steve and I were out of pot and had decided to get some more. For some reason we left in a car with four friends of his. I say friends, but these guys were members of a serious gang. Steve and I were in the backseat making out when I noticed we had pulled off the interstate into a secluded area near a bike path.

I remember seeing a tunnel of running water next to the bike path, but before I knew it, Steve and I were having sex. After, he handed me a pill and told me to take it. I wasn't so drunk that I would have taken just anything, and I was very upset and embarrassed that we had had sex in the presence of these other guys. I said no to the pill and remember telling Steve that I needed to get home, that my grandma would be mad if I was late, but it was to no avail.

The next thing I knew, Steve pulled out a knife and held it to my neck. I was forced to swallow the pill (which I later learned was Ecstasy) before each of the other four guys took their turn with me inside the car. They were very rough and I began to bleed, badly, all over the interior of the car. By this time I was in a very odd state of consciousness and unconsciousness. Maybe it was the drug, or maybe it was my mind mercifully distancing me from this horrible thing that was happening.

All I remember after that is a blur of police officers. That memory, in turn, ran into a memory of my being in the hospital. How I got to the hospital I have no idea. But I did. As I suspected, Grandma had indeed gotten worried, but in a different way than I expected. She had called the police and reported me as a runaway. It may be that a police cruiser found me and took me in. I don't know for sure.

At the hospital they tested me for semen and drugs, and I was given the full rape workup. I really didn't want to let anyone near my privates, so the rape workup in itself was quite traumatic. I can also just imagine what I must have looked like. I had lost the baby—I had been fourteen weeks pregnant and I am sure all of the adults around me felt that loss was for the best. While I did feel relief, there was a lot of grief, sadness, and anger, too. That baby was a human life I made with a boy I loved and now he or she would never be born. The way I was drinking and smoking pot I might have lost the baby eventually anyway, but that's something I will not know until I meet God.

At some point my grandma came to get me. We later went to Walmart and got a new purse and some clothes, and then headed to the police station to give a statement. I hoped to get validation from the police officers, to get a warrant out for these thugs and get them off the street. If they had raped me, they had done it to others—and would again.

I was to be hugely disappointed. Hopefully police officers today are more sensitive than the cop who asked me, "Why are you ruining those boys' lives? You need to drop this." I had told officials who the boys were and they'd had time to get their story straight before they were questioned. Their story was that "I wanted it," that I begged and teased them so much that they finally gave in. I called the cop a really bad name before walking out the door. I don't remember going back to Grandma's house, but she must have driven me.

The things that were running through my mind were insane. Just a year before I had falsely implied that my own father had raped me, and there was a part of me that felt that because I had not told the full truth about that, I deserved this rape. In addition, until hours before I had thought that Steve was my best friend, but the boys who raped me were his friends, so how could that be? I definitely had not wanted to have sex with those boys, but I also didn't want to ruin their lives, as I had my father's. I decided that the best thing to do was to get my butt home and try to forget about it all.

But I will never forget what happened that day. One of the big after-results of the rape was that I now had zero boundaries with men. Through the rape they took whatever little bit of self-esteem, whatever tiny ounce of self-respect I had. I felt that I was nothing, deserved nothing. My body was sore; my psyche was shattered. I was grieving for my baby and for the loss of whatever tiny bit of innocence I'd had left, and I was furious with the police. To top it off I was hugely disillusioned with Steve.

Grandma decided that I didn't need to see any of my friends, so I moped around the house and tried to make sense of my life. But I couldn't. What I really wanted was to go home, but it struck me that I didn't know where home was, or if I even had one. My dad had sent me to my mother; my mother had sent me to my grandmother. Where was I to go from here?

Ten

★

True Love

The aftereffects of sexual abuse affect my life every day. Even now, the abuse can still pop into the forefront of my mind without a moment's notice. It gives me a sick feeling in the pit of my stomach, and I have to dig deep to remind myself that I am no longer that young girl. I am strong. I have value. I contribute positively to the world.

It took me awhile, but I now understand that I cannot change my past. I also had to realize that I did nothing wrong and sometimes that tempts me to play the victim. One day recently I woke up with the victim mind-set and I knew I had to put it aside. I cannot— do not—allow victimization to control my life. I also know that I could easily get lost in that kind of negative thinking.

Instead, when I woke up that morning, I thought, *So what? Now what?* I know everything happens for a reason, and I trust that God will someday let me know why my early years were tough. Maybe the reason was so I could write this book and empower other parents to better watch over their children, or for young people to know that they have options even though they might have to search far and wide to find them.

That morning, when I began the negative self-talk that happens with the victim mind-set, I distracted myself by doing something fun. I love hiking but didn't have time for a run up Koko Head, the crater near my home. Instead, I reveled in my kids and after Abbie went off to school and Mady was settled with my brother Nick, I paddle boarded my way to work. All the way I repeated to myself that I am not a victim. Instead, I am a survivor.

Being a survivor wasn't how I felt after the rape, however. I felt that I had been destroyed mentally, physically, and emotionally. Any sense of a positive body image I might have had was completely lost, and I came to feel that all I was good for was as a tool for men. Several days after the incident I called my dad, who lived about half an hour away, to ask if I could visit. This was the first time I had seen Dad since I had let people believe that he raped me, and he treated me kind of like you would a pet snake. I understood why, but I really craved my dad just then. I just wanted him to wrap his arms around me and hug me tight like he used to when I was little. Unfortunately, my inability to make a good decision when I was a child will affect my family relationships for the rest of our lives.

Before I could set foot into Dad's house, though, he took me to his lawyer's office so I could say on tape that I lied. Other than that one incidence, Dad and I have never talked about why I didn't correct the adults when they thought Dad molested me. I have wanted to bring up the subject over and over again to tell him how regretful I am, but have never been able to do that. It was all so complicated and I was so young. Somehow I could never find the words.

I knew I could never face Nathan again under any circumstances and am deeply sorry and regretful that it all turned out the way it did. I never meant to hurt my dad or anyone else.

Now when I told my dad about the gang rape, I could see all the conflicted "Dad" emotions play across his face. Then he said he wanted to go out and take care of it himself, so we got into the car and went out to look for the boys. I guess it was a good thing we didn't find them because I think Dad would have ripped them to shreds.

While my dad was sympathetic and helpful, Beth was skeptical that the rape had happened at all. I realize now that when I accused my dad of raping me that I hurt Beth, too. As a consequence, I believe Beth thought I lied about the boys and what they did to me.

While I was disappointed in Beth's reaction, I understood it. I recall many instances where I clashed badly with Beth when she behaved toward me in a manner that I now understand she believed was in my best interests. Today we have an uneasy relationship, but are closer than we have been in the past. Our goals today are often the same, and this includes putting family first. We just have very different ways of getting there.

Since all this happened I have gained a lot of perspective and maturity and realize how important it is not only to be fully truthful about important matters, but also to be very clear when you communicate with another person. Miscommunication is the source of many arguments and disagreements that could be avoided if each person was clear about what the other person said and felt. As you've seen through my experience, situations that lack truth and clarity can get out of hand and can damage friendships and family relationships forever.

★

I had originally been sent to Colorado to have my baby and give him or her up for adoption. As neither of those things was going to happen, I was bounced back to Alaska. Shortly after I moved back, my mother and I got into a huge fight about her new boyfriend, John Greene. John was ex-military and was from North Carolina. He was the kind of guy who, at night, often used our shared hallway bathroom while nude. That made me very uncomfortable, but when I mentioned my feelings to my mother she said, "You are *not* going to accuse another man of *any*thing." I had no intention of accusing John. His nakedness, especially right after the rape, just made me nervous. Besides, my mother had known him for only a few weeks, and here he was living with us.

Our words escalated from there, and my mother felt we'd all be better off if I moved in with her ex-boyfriend, Jimmy Neeley. Fortunately he agreed. At the time, Jimmy lived with his father, brother, and several other guys. For obvious reasons he knew that arrangement would not work if I was brought into the mix, so he found a house for the two of us.

Jimmy offered me a more stable environment than I'd had with my mother and even set up some loose rules that I had to follow, such as a curfew.

Even though I still attended school regularly and maintained semi-good grades, I had become a girl who ditched class as often as she could. I also no longer participated in any extracurricular activities, such as sports. Instead, I smoked pot all the time and had become the free, crazy, bad girl every parent loves to hate. I was such a product of my environment that I felt (like my mother, sister, and girlfriends) that I needed to be in a sexual relationship if I was to have any value as a person. But I also desperately wanted to be a mom with a family of my own. I was so tired of all the dysfunction in my family that in my child mind I thought I could create a new family filled with love and peace. That's why I think I was so attracted to a man from Fairbanks who hung in our circle named Brendan.

I met Brendan at a party and I remember the party specifically because it was the first time I had tried cocaine. I had always shied away from it before, because the drug had turned my dad into a stranger, but several people there convinced me to try it. Brendan was ten years older than I, which put him at twenty-three. I was so ready to let an "older" man take care of me that I fell head over heels in love. I was strongly attracted to the fact that he was quiet. He was also kind and loving, and he treated me well. When he told me he loved me I was overwhelmed by the need to love him back, without judgment, without question. Another part of the attraction was Brendan's daughter, Kira, who was about six at the time.

Kira was an adorable little girl who lived with her mother (who had given birth to Kira when she was just seventeen), but she spent a few weekends a month with Brendan when he wasn't working at the gold mines. Kira was a beautiful blonde with brown eyes. She loved it when I did her hair, and I remember that we colored and played games. Brendan seemed to be such a good father; here it was, my ready-made family!

Jimmy trusted me with Brendan, but because Brendan was so much older, we kept our relationship secret from everyone else. Even I knew about statutory rape laws. I knew Brendan did, too, because after the first time we slept together he put his hand on my face and said, "Shhhhh. Don't tell anyone."

Brendan even encouraged me to get a "boyfriend," for appearances sake. I found a great guy who lived in town and we became good friends. We didn't have much of a physical relationship because I was so in love with Brendan, but we had a lot of fun spending time together. I was so hooked on Brendan it was almost like Stockholm syndrome. It really was sick.

Brendan and I often did cocaine together and he played the

song "Shaggy Angel" over and over. "That's our song," he'd say. Why he targeted me, I don't know. Maybe it was because I looked so much older than I was; I had neither the body nor the mind of someone my age. At eighteen, Barbara was always asked for her identification when she tried to buy cigarettes. At thirteen, I never was asked. Now I look at my daughter Abbie, and my little sister, Bonnie Jo, and think no way. No way would I ever condone anything close to this kind of relationship for them.

The summer of my fourteenth year Brendan and I became very close. My mother was wrapped up in John, so my younger brother, Nick, hung with us at least four nights a week. I didn't see Barbara as much because I now preferred to spend time with Brendan rather than go to all the parties she attended. Plus Barbara and our friend Danika had moved to Fairbanks and didn't come to Anderson very often. My brother Tucker was still bouncing back and forth between our dad and mother, but this would be his last summer in Alaska. After that he never returned. Brendan eventually started staying with Jimmy and me. Jimmy didn't allow us to mess around at his house, so we either went to a friend's house or down to the river in Brendan's truck when we wanted to be intimate.

One evening, late, Barbara stopped by to pick up her dogs. She had come through Anderson earlier in the evening on her way to a party and dropped her dogs off with me. When Barbara picked up the dogs it was obvious that she had been drinking, but someone else was driving, so I was not worried about her getting home. I should have been. Since then I have realized that where there is smoke there is fire. I should have figured out that if Barbara was drunk, probably the people she was with were drunk, too.

The next morning there was a knock on our door. A neighbor who was also an EMT had heard on her emergency scanner that Barbara had been in a car accident and that the vehicle was upside down in four feet of swamp water. I was frantic with worry as Brendan drove me the ninety miles to the hospital in Fairbanks. When we arrived, I was horrified to find Barbara with a deep gash over one eye. I was so mad at the man who had been driving that I stormed into his hospital room but settled down when I saw that he had dozens of staples in his head.

This was my first experience with the reality of drinking and driving, and the tragedy it can cause. The result was that I realized how much I cared for my sister. I remembered how diligently she had looked out for me when I was small, and how young she was when she did that. The memory made me want to cry. In recent years we had both become so involved in our own dysfunction that we had been too busy to see how much the other was hurting. That, I decided, was going to change.

★

In September 2001 I once again found myself pregnant. I remembered how my mother had reacted the last time I was expecting so I wanted to avoid another scene like that at all costs. I was confused. On the one hand, I really wanted to be a mom.

Me at age four months. Don't you love the ugly striped couch? *(Photograph courtesy of Lyssa Chapman)*

All dressed up for my kindergarten photo. *(Photograph courtesy of Lyssa Chapman)*

I recently went back to visit my elementary school in Waikiki. I loved attending this school! *(Photograph by Lisa Wysocky)*

This is the door to the room at the Hostel where my mother stayed before Nick was born. I am standing in the indoor courtyard. *(Photograph by Lisa Wysocky)*

The two-bedroom apartment at the Waipuna was a big step up from our one-room studio. *(Photograph by Lisa Wysocky)*

By sixth grade I had long stopped believing in Santa, but I still liked the symbolism of Christmas and the holidays. *(Photograph courtesy of Lyssa Chapman)*

My seventh-grade photo. I felt nothing like the other kids in my class. *(Photograph courtesy of Lyssa Chapman)*

> *How do you think the sexual abuse is affecting you right now?*

Sexual abuse is affecting my trust in other people. I feel asthough I can't get too close to anyone cuz' I'll never know what they will do. And it affects my vision of the world, I thought all people were nice but now I think most people are out to get me.

Sexual Abuse Is a Trauma

> *Look up the word trauma in the dictionary. Write the definition below.*

Trauma: A disastrous event outside the range of usual experience as rape, military combat, or an airplane crash.

In counseling I found that writing out my thoughts helped. Reading this now makes me feel very sad. *(Photograph courtesy of Lyssa Chapman)*

> *In what ways do you think that sexual abuse is a trauma?*

For me its a trauma because people joke about rape a lot & I don't give the responce they want me to & they think I'm strange. Plus I can't sleep sometimes, I have nightmares & I don't feel safe

More writing from my counseling workbook. Every child deserves to feel safe, but that wasn't the case for me. *(Photograph courtesy of Lyssa Chapman)*

The beginning of my "bad girl" years. I can't believe I thought I looked cool. *(Photograph courtesy of Lyssa Chapman)*

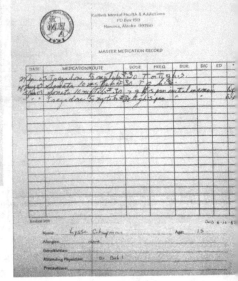

A prescription for just one of the many
medications prescribed to me. *(Photograph
courtesy of Lyssa Chapman)*

The medication list grows and grows.
(Photograph courtesy of Lyssa Chapman)

Barbara, our mother, and me, just
after Abbie's birth. My mother seems
thrilled with her grandchildren, Travis
(left) and Abbie *(right)*. *(Photograph
courtesy of Lyssa Chapman)*

Abbie and me. Cute clothes, but I hate
the photo. I was fifteen years old. No
child that young should have a baby.
(Photograph courtesy of Lyssa Chapman)

When I moved back to Hawai'i (both times) I moved into this house with Dad and his family. *(Photograph by Lisa Wysocky)*

Abbie and I had so much fun together. *(Photograph courtesy of Lyssa Chapman)*

ADAM BOUSKA

This unusual photo was taken to support the NOH8 Campaign. This nonprofit organization's mission is to promote equality. *Left to right:* Leland, Duane Lee, Dad, Beth, and me. *(Photograph courtesy of Adam Bouska)*

On the set of *Dog the Bounty Hunter*. This is actually part of Dad's office at Da Kine Bail Bonds in Honolulu. *(Photograph by Lisa Wysocky)*

One of the best things about being part of a show like *Dog the Bounty Hunter* are the charitable opportunities that come our way. Here we are at a 2008 CORE charity event to defeat racism in Kahala, Hawai'i. *Left to right:* Niger Innis of CORE, Duane "Dog" Chapman, Beth Smith Chapman, Leland Chapman, me, and Duane Lee Chapman. *(Photograph courtesy of Mona Wood-Sword)*

I loved my dad-and-daughter dance at my wedding reception. *(Photograph courtesy of Ana Cordova)*

I love basketball, both playing and watching. Here I am between Leland (*left*) and Duane Lee (*right*). *(Photograph courtesy of Mona Wood-Sword)*

Cecily and me. I love this girl beyond words. *(Photograph courtesy of Lyssa Chapman)*

My "self-portrait." Actually I was just goofing around on my iPhone. *(Photograph courtesy of Lyssa Chapman)*

When Beth and I heard The Rock was filming less than a block away from Dad's house, we had to go down to meet him. *(Photograph courtesy of Lyssa Chapman)*

My girls and I love to have fun outdoors. *(Photograph courtesy of Lyssa Chapman)*

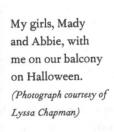

My girls, Mady and Abbie, with me on our balcony on Halloween. *(Photograph courtesy of Lyssa Chapman)*

On the other, I had grown up enough in the past year or so that I realized I was way too young. I am not proud of the fact that I pounded on my stomach for a month every morning before school when I was in the shower. I had also heard of a girl who lost her baby after doing cocaine, so I did massive amounts of the drug—so much, in fact, that I regularly threw up at school.

I was so scared that I didn't tell anyone. I told Brendan when I was twelve weeks along, and I still remember how shocked I was when he suggested I give up the baby for adoption. I had not intentionally gotten pregnant, but like most girls, once I was, I had hoped that the father would embrace the pregnancy. I wanted us to be a family.

I hid my news from everyone else until I was six months along. During the fall and winter in Alaska that isn't hard to do, as everyone bundles up in lots of sweaters. But one cold February day after I had thrown up at school my counselor came in and asked if I was expecting. I nodded that I was, and she convinced me that I had to tell my mother.

That wasn't as easy as it sounded, however. A month or so before, Barbara had announced that she was pregnant, and our mother had totally flipped out. By this time Barbara had moved to Anchorage with her boyfriend, Travis Mimms. Anchorage was about three hundred miles and more than five hours away. To make matters worse, we had just found out that the dog Barbara had left with our mother before she moved was expecting. I remember asking my mother lots of questions about pregnancy, pretending I was curious about the dog but really wondering what was going on in my own body.

I knew our mother would not be pleased to hear yet that another person was pregnant, so in hopes of softening her reaction I met her after school with my counselor. My counselor had convinced me that I needed medical attention and that I needed to tell my mother. Besides, I was really starting to show. I had gotten so good at hiding the pregnancy, however, even to the point of putting "used" tampons in the trash every month to try to fool Jimmy, that my mother was quite disbelieving when I spilled the news.

Because I was so underage I was afraid Brendan would get in trouble if people knew he was the father, so for weeks I told everyone I had met a guy from Anchorage at a party—a one-night stand. I'm not sure how many people believed me, but I think John and my mother did.

My counselor did not, however. She had suspected that Brendan and I were having an inappropriate relationship and had reported him multiple times to authorities—who had done nothing.

Later, John, my mother, and I agreed that it would be best if I moved in with them until the baby was born. We also decided that I would give the baby up for adoption, but I wanted the baby to have a good start, and that meant prenatal care. Two other events also figured into this decision. The first was that Brendan worked in the gold mines and was often away for up to three months at a time. He was just getting ready to leave again and would not be around as I moved closer to my due date. The other was that Jimmy was so far behind on the rent that he was about to be evicted. I was just so happy that my mom wanted me I think I would have moved back no matter what. Despite her choices in life I loved her and had missed her.

I was just coming to terms with all of this when the school called to say that because I was pregnant, I could not come back to classes. They felt I was a bad influence on the other students, so they set me up with a Mac laptop at home, and I finished ninth grade in my mother's living room. I didn't know it then, but that was also the end of my formal education.

Eleven

★

Babyhood

I am so grateful for the faith I have now, so grateful for God's love. And I love raising my children by God's word. Abbie and Mady regularly attend Sunday school and on Friday nights Abbie goes to A.W.A.N.A. club at our local church. A.W.A.N.A. is a great organization that helps churches and parents work together to develop spiritually strong children and youth. My girls and I say our prayers every night before we go to bed, and we bless all of our family members and friends. I am so happy that the love of God runs pure through my little family each day.

It used to be that I was so wrapped up in the drama of my life that I couldn't see the forest for the trees. I had no idea how far off track I was. I should have been enjoying my high school years, but I was a long way from that. I also was a long way from my days as a member of Pastor Jeremiah's congregation and from the times when we'd sit as a family and listen as Dad read us Bible stories.

So where was God in my life? The real question should be where was I with God? I'm sorry to say I didn't give Him much thought then, although I can look back and see that He was protecting me. As bad as events in my life were, if God had not been there, life could have been much worse. If He hadn't been there, I'm not sure I would have survived the next few years. I do not know why these things have happened to me, but I do know that because I went through them—and survived them—it has given me a great deal of drive to prevent the same experiences from happening to other girls.

★

Somehow I knew that three ideal things for an expectant mom to have during her pregnancy were peace, love, and support. I didn't have much of any of that. First was the question of the baby's father. My mother and John asked me several times if Brendan was the dad. I still didn't want Brendan to get in trouble, so I said no, but I think by then that everyone knew he was. When I finally told the truth, my mother got so mad that she again threw me out of the house.

By this time I was more than seven months pregnant. I had done a lot of research online about what was going on inside my body and how the baby was developing. Once I educated myself in this area I knew I could never give my baby up. In addition to understanding on a whole new level that my baby was a real person growing inside me, I had fallen completely in love with my unborn child.

The decision to keep my baby was the first "adult" decision I ever made. It seemed as if all of the adults in my life had already decided that I was going to give up the baby, but this decision was one I could control. I rationalized it this way: I sometimes explain that an accident is something bad that you don't want, but a surprise is something wonderful you didn't know you wanted until you got it. My unborn child was my wonderful surprise.

Could an adoptive family have given my child more than I could as a teen mom? Probably. But I vowed then and there that from this point on I would devote my life to making the best life I could for my baby. I knew no one could love this child more than I could. I also knew that I didn't have many good role models in the mothering department, but I took the best of what I had from my mother, Tawny, the nannies, and Beth, and built my parenting foundation from there. I also knew from the many instances of negative parenting what I didn't want to do as a mother.

One thing I knew from watching all the television I had at my dad's house was how much the women on TV loved their children. I remember in particular a movie called *For Keeps* that had a teen mom as the main character. I also remember several Lifetime movies, episodes of *Cold Case Files,* and other shows that dealt with women and their children. I learned a lot of my parenting skills from those TV moms.

There would be many times that I slipped or made mistakes and the challenges were often overwhelming, but keeping my child was by far the best decision I have ever made. I also want to state that my decision was the best for *my* baby and *me,* and not necessarily the best decision for someone else.

The night my mother threw me out I stayed with my friend Danika, who was back in Anderson. The next day I saw John in his Suburban in the parking lot. As I walked closer I saw that he was crying. "Your mother and I want to talk to you," he said through his tears.

When we got to our trailer, it turned out that my mother was drunk. She and John sobbed about what a huge disappointment and embarrassment I was to them. What were they going to do with me? How would they deal with this problem I had caused? As you have seen, my mother and I had a rocky and complicated relationship, as many teen girls do with their moms—but the addition of drugs, alcohol, and sex made the combination of the relationship and the situation into a mess bigger than either of us knew how to handle. Or so I thought. It turned out that John and my mother had a plan.

Their plan was that I would move to Alabama and marry Brendan. My mother had gotten on our trusty computer to find that I was of legal age to marry in that state. Then she drew a map that showed me how to find my way there. She also handed me a letter she had written that gave her consent to the marriage, just in case I needed it. The last part of the plan was that while I could return to Alaska when I was sixteen, I had to leave right then.

I felt so bad. While I may have been a huge disappointment to my mother, it didn't help that she actively let me know what an embarrassment I was to her and that she wanted me to go so far away. I was ashamed enough without her pointing out all my many mistakes—many of which she had a part in. I mean, what kind of mother gives her daughter illegal drugs? This also was a time when positive reinforcement about making the best of a really bad situation would have helped. A "let's find the best solution for you and the baby" plan rather than an "out of sight, out of mind" plan.

There were obviously lots of problems with my mother's idea to move me to Alabama, but the first was that Brendan was working in the gold mines and I didn't know how to reach him. He was due back in several weeks, so until that time I stayed with Danika. When Brendan returned he happily agreed to the plan and to the marriage, so we headed south. I was so in love. I held Brendan's hand the entire way as I imagined the farm we would live on in Alabama.

The next glitch in the plan, however, put a stop to it entirely. When Brendan and I reached the Canadian border Brendan got out of the car to deal with border officials while I stayed put. A few minutes later he returned and said, "We're not getting through here. I knew this wasn't going to work." It turned out that we needed a passport and I didn't have one.

When I called my mother she said I wasn't her problem anymore and to have a nice life. Again, words can be so hurtful, and I became so distraught by these words in particular. With nowhere to go I went back to stay with Danika, who was nineteen and living on her own. She seemed happy to let me stay with her and even gave some baby clothes to me as a gift. I liked staying there; life with Danika was peaceful.

★

Several weeks later Barbara called. She had been living with Dad and Beth, who had moved to Hawai'i, but had recently had another fight with them and wanted to come back to Alaska. Our friends and I bought her a ticket, and Brendan and I picked her up in Anchorage.

I had not told Barbara that I was pregnant because my mother did not want Dad to know. My mother figured Dad would never find out if I gave the baby up for adoption. But Barbara had discovered what was going on when she called the school looking for me and they told her I was not in school because I was expecting. Barbara then called our mother and yelled that she tried to tell her multiple times that Brendan and I were having a relationship.

Barbara also was expecting and was due in May, while my due date was June 18. I was really looking forward to going through the birth and parenting experiences with Barbara. Our closeness of recent years had continued to grow, and she had once again become the big sister I looked to for advice.

When Barbara came back to Alaska, she moved in with our mother and Nick. John had taken a job ninety miles away, in Fairbanks, and was rarely there. One day I went to visit Barbara and was surprised to see how happy our mother was about the prospect of being a grandmother to both of our babies. This was a huge turn of events and a development I had a hard time getting my head around. The end result was that I moved back in with my mother, and life for the next few weeks was good.

Even though Barbara was not due until May, in April she lost her mucus plug and her doctor felt she needed to be close to a hospital until the baby arrived. In Anderson we were nearly two hours away. Hospital staff made arrangements for Barbara and me to stay at a hotel near the hospital, and we made ourselves comfortable while we waited for the baby to come. That happened a lot quicker than anyone expected.

At the end of April 2002, Barbara went into labor prematurely and gave birth to her son, Travis Drake-Lee Chapman, on the twenty-seventh. I was honored to be in the delivery room with Barbara and am so blessed to have gone through the birth with her and Travis. While Barbara recovered in the hospital, Mom, John, Nick, and I stayed in the hotel room until she and Travis were ready to go home. Medicaid paid all the costs for the room; otherwise we could not have afforded to stay there.

I had been in touch with Brendan all this time and had told him where we were staying. I had even found ways to see him occasionally, even though every adult I knew had forbidden contact between us. One evening John was in the bar next door getting some food and cash for Barbara and me. When he saw Brendan's truck go by he got drunk and then called the police—

although they never showed up. In the eyes of John and my mother, Brendan had taken advantage of my youth, repeatedly raped me, and needed to be arrested.

At this point I had been with Brendan for about two years and I still loved him with all my heart. From the beginning of my pregnancy he encouraged me to tell the truth. I was the one who had not wanted to name my baby's father because I wanted to protect him. I knew in some way that a relationship with a young teen and a grown man was improper, but Brendan was a bright, kind light in my world of dysfunction. Was our relationship wrong? Absolutely, totally, completely. But I still loved him.

After Travis was born we all went back to our mother's house in Anderson, but our mother stayed only a week or so before she decided to move in with John in Fairbanks. It was too bad, especially because Barbara at twenty was so not ready to be a mother. Young babies need love and care from their parents twenty-four hours a day, seven days a week. There is no time for anything else, and when there is no dad in the picture, it all falls to the mom. Barbara could not handle the pressure, and when Travis was three weeks old she took some hallucinogenic mushrooms, which meant she could no longer breast-feed. From that day on, I was the one who was responsible for Travis's care. I was still just fourteen.

The day of Travis's six-week checkup was June 10, my fifteenth birthday. I really wanted to have my baby on my birthday, so when we got to Fairbanks for Travis's appointment Barbara went to the store and got some castor oil. We had heard that if I drank enough of this it would hurry the baby along, and maybe it did. Halfway home I went into labor and we turned the car around.

I was definitely not prepared for the birth experience. The pain was excruciating, and my mother was nowhere to be found. At the hospital we learned that their one anesthesiologist was at the scene of an accident, so no one was available to give me an epidural. I also had not taken any Lamaze classes. None was offered, and I didn't know enough to seek them out. In fact, I never realized that any kind of childbirth class existed. By this time I was screaming so loudly that Barbara dropped to her knees and began to pray.

We had gotten to the hospital at about eight in the evening. When the doctor finally came in to examine me just after midnight, he said two words that no one in labor ever needs to hear, "Uh-oh." Apparently I was fully dilated and my baby was coming right now! The anesthesiologist had arrived, as had my mother and Danika, but my baby's heart rate dropped dramatically and there was no time for an epidural. Instead, someone found a suction cup and the doctor pulled my baby out.

Abbie Mae Chapman was born eleven minutes after 1:00 a.m. on June 11, a little more than an hour after my fifteenth birthday was over. I'll always remember how completely beautiful Abbie was, and still is. I had hoped for a girl, and the few baby clothes I had gathered together or been given were pink. When Travis was born, he had gotten too cold right after his birth. That may have been because he was a preemie, but I was so worried that would happen to my little Abbie, too. But it didn't.

Right after the birth I breast-fed Abbie, and I watched in the nursery as my baby was cleaned up. When they handed her back to me I realized that once I left the hospital no one was going to help me take care of her; Abbie's every need would have to be filled by me, and me alone. Even though a social worker had visited me in the hospital to try to prepare me, I had no idea how daunting that would be.

★

Back at home in Anderson I found that with Travis and Abbie so close in age it was almost like having twins. They even pooped and napped on the same schedule. I was so in love with them both. I was sad that my mother was not there, as I would have loved to have my baby's grandmother closer.

That fall I tried to go back to school. I was too young to get a driver's license so I walked back and forth. No one initially told me about pumping and storing my breast milk. When I finally did learn about that option I thought it was such a great idea that I stole a breast pump. If I could store my milk, then maybe Barbara could feed Abbie while I was at school. Unfortunately, the pump seemed to be missing the suction part. I felt bad about stealing the pump, but there was no money for one in our meager budget. It quickly became too hard to leave school several times a day to go home to feed Abbie and still get in enough class time. After those first few sporadic weeks of tenth grade, I never went back.

Babyhood

During this time life was quiet and somewhat routine. In fact, life was as normal as it had been for me since the time I lived with Dad and Tawny before Dad started taking drugs. That is, life was normal if you consider two young unwed girls, their younger brother, and their babies living in a trailer in Alaska normal. Yes, our mother had left Nick with us. Apparently there was not room for him in the one-room construction barracks she and John lived in.

As much as I adored my sister, I understood that Barbara was as unreliable as the men in our lives and that she had her own struggles. I often think about why people become addicts, and there are about as many reasons as there are people. Many individuals, however, have an underlying mental illness such as depression or bipolar disorder that is not being treated, and sometimes they drift toward alcohol or illegal street drugs. Barbara may have been one of these people. While she partied less than usual during this time, it was still too much, and Travis's care still fell to me. Parenting is time-consuming and takes a lot of dedication and responsibility. I know Barbara loved Travis with everything she had, but she was not ready for motherhood on a day-to-day, hour-by-hour basis. I still don't know how I was able to care for two newborns while I was still so young.

Today, in spite of my love for both of my daughters, I do not recommend teen pregnancy and willingly offer up my story (the part you've already read and the parts to come) as a cautionary tale. I feel strongly that our media and television programming glamorize the idea, and allow lost young women like me to fantasize about creating their own perfect families. I'm here to tell you that the fantasy is never close to reality, and raising a child while you are still a child yourself is the hardest thing in the world to do.

Twelve

★

Sweet Dreams Are Not Always
as They Seem

As an adult, I gladly take responsibility for my life. I pay the
bills, get my children to school, and make sure dinner is on
the table every night.

Recently I attended a Smart Business Hawai'i dinner and found
myself in a room with the owners of many successful independent
businesses in the state along with a Honolulu mayoral candidate. I
was there because my business partner and I had just opened up No
Tan Lines, our new tanning salon that features red light therapy.
Earlier in the day I had been busy designing fliers, budgeting our
next few months, and dealing with an electrical problem, and
that evening I felt I could completely relate to business talk that
surrounded the dinner tables.

One thing that came up over and over was my age—or lack of it. Even though I am just twenty-five, I feel that I have the experience of someone who is thirty-five or forty, because even though it is a shoulder load of adult responsibility to open a new business, it is hard for me to remember a time when I haven't had that kind of obligation.

When my mother left, full responsibility for the mortgage on the trailer had fallen to Barbara and me. Until that point I had been paying rent to my mother so Abbie and I could live there. The mortgage was right at $500 a month, plus there were expenses for electricity, diapers, and other essentials. I don't know what we would have done had Barbara not qualified for both welfare and food stamps. Plus she was able to get these benefits for our babies, Nick, and the two of us. Otherwise we would not have had either food or shelter.

Even though Barbara and I were now moms, we were still kids, and unsupervised kids at that. After a big party we threw, one of the neighbors called our mother to tell her what we were up to. The trailer was so messy after the party that our mother told us we needed to find a new place and that she was locking up the house.

Barbara and I moved a few blocks down the road to Second and D Streets, to an even more run-down trailer. This trailer didn't even have any working plumbing, and only part of the house had heat. Plus sewage backed up into it. We struggled along for a few months and barely kept our heads above water before Barbara threw in the towel and called Dad. Almost before I knew what was happening Barbara and Travis moved to Hawai'i and in with Dad and Beth, while Nick moved back with our mother in Fairbanks.

That's how I found myself at fifteen with the responsibility of paying the rent and providing food for Abbie and myself. Because I was not yet eighteen I did not qualify for food stamps or other such services on my own. Plus I had essentially been abandoned by both my mother and sister, the two women who could have provided things that I needed. Not yet sixteen, I could not find a job, and in a little town like Anderson, Alaska, there were few options for child care. I should have been panicked with terror. How would I pay the rent? Feed us? Keep us warm? By this time it was winter and I don't have to tell you how cold winters are in Alaska. Instead, I was resigned. I just felt that this was where life had led me, and in a way I had part of the life I had wanted—I had the house to myself, and it was quiet.

Looking back I should have been angry—at my mother, at Barbara, at Brendan, even at myself. But there was no time for that. I was in full survival mode, and I was determined to do just that.

I knew I had to live by the equation of a job + money = rent. I also realized that if I had trouble finding people to care for Abbie while I looked for a job, others might have trouble finding people to watch their children while they worked. The next morning I went to the Dew Drop Inn and was thrilled to find several people in there drinking while their kids tagged along. Great! I thought. Instant kids to take care of. I obviously wasn't a licensed day care provider, even though some of the children spent time in my trailer, but I loved kids and took good care of each one. All my playtime nurturing my dolls when I was younger finally paid off!

In addition to taking care of all the kids, I found there was a lot of work involved in living in that run-down trailer. I washed our clothes in the sink and hung them to dry on a string I had run in front of the woodstove. I used the woodstove a lot because the trailer had a furnace that ran on diesel gas, and gas cost money that I didn't have.

Fortunately, Jimmy had dropped off several cords of wood in the form of logs, so every day I chopped up those logs and fed them to the woodstove. I have to say that chopping wood just to stay warm changes your priorities in a hurry. What's on television that night no longer matters, nor does whatever the current hit song is on the radio. Politics, current events, even local gossip, none of it is of any importance . . . except for the weather. I kept up on the weather because if a blizzard was headed our way I needed to stock up on more wood. In short, whatever time I didn't spend taking care of Abbie or the other kids, I spent keeping the trailer (and us) clean, warm, and dry. Poverty would have been a step up.

I am very proud that I was always able to pay the rent, in spite of the hustling I had to do to get it. Abbie never missed a meal, and our clothes were as clean as they could be, considering our limitations. I was constantly on the lookout for ways to become more efficient in my daily chores, and after a while I had them down to a science.

This kind of life was not what I expected when I found out I was pregnant. No teen can possibly look into the future or consider all the challenges one has to conquer when you have to support a baby. Did I think my mother and sister would leave me? No. Did I think I'd have to find my own heat and food? No. Did I ever possibly consider that I'd have to pay rent or that I wasn't old enough to get a job? Of course not. I'm not sure what I thought other than a vague notion that Brendan and I would be together with our baby, but I had none of the details or contingencies worked out in my mind.

Adult pressures rained down onto me, but I held my own quite well until the day Abbie got sick. I breast-fed Abbie for the first year or so, but she had acid reflux and one day began projectile vomiting. I couldn't get her to keep anything down and was so scared. I took her to the hospital but rather than focusing solely on Abbie, the medical staff there wanted to run drug tests on me. The next thing I knew a representative from Child Protective Services was in the room, and I had immediate flashbacks to the horrible time when CPS tried to separate me from my dad. I grabbed Abbie from the nurse and turned to leave, but the CPS representative said that while I was free to leave, I had to leave Abbie there. There was not the remotest possibility that I was going to leave without my daughter, so I squeezed past them through the door and went home.

Three days later a different CPS representative knocked on my door. I knew if I didn't let him in nothing would ever get resolved, so I opened the door, even though my heart was about thumping through my chest. He looked around the trailer, then spent a little time with Abbie while I watched. I was so afraid that I don't even remember breathing.

Eventually he said, "You're a good mom. Your place is clean, and your daughter is well fed and has a good place to sleep. You're very young and I wish you had more help, but you and your daughter are both doing okay."

When I heard those words my knees began to shake and I wanted to cry with relief, but somehow I held my emotions together until he left. Then I grabbed Abbie and hugged her long and hard.

I remained in a state of increased anxiety from the caseworker's presence in my home long after he went away. I also remembered that Dad's anxiety was so strong after the CPS struggles we had in Hawai'i when I was a child that he kept me out of school for a year. He was that afraid that they'd come back and take me from him. Now I knew just how he felt.

Dad, however, had the option of sending Barbara and Tucker away and of moving me to a different home so that I would be harder to find. I didn't have those resources or options and instead held all my fears tightly inside me. Eventually it all became too much and I am sorry to say that I began hanging with friends who used drugs. Before long I was using cocaine again and having a lot of casual sex.

★

I was so relieved when Barbara returned not too long after this following yet another fight with Dad and Beth. Thank goodness Barbara applied for and received Section 8 housing, and we all moved into a three-bedroom town house in Fairbanks with our babies, who were now more than a year old.

I was so glad to be moving from the worn-out trailer into a much nicer home, but sad that I had to leave a lot of our furniture. We had recently purchased a van, and the only way we could move any of the furniture to Barbara's and my new home was to put the smaller pieces of furniture in the van. We had to leave the bigger items, such as the mattresses. Between the two of us, we had enough gas money for only two vanloads. We packed the most important pieces and left the rest. By the time we came back for the second load later in the day the trailer had gotten so cold that our beloved pet birds had frozen to death.

That was in 2003, and no one has lived in that trailer since. The trailer is just not livable. In fact, all of the stuff we left is still there. A few months ago a friend went in, found some photos we had left behind, and sent them to me. While I appreciated the gesture very much I tore up all the photos. They were just too depressing.

★

Once we settled into Fairbanks I got my very first job. I was a cashier at a McDonald's. I say first job but this really is the only "job" I ever had for any length of time. I worked days while

Barbara took care of the kids. Barbara had found a job waitressing at a bar, so she worked nights while I took my turn caring for Abbie and Travis. The problem was that Barbara often drank away any money she made waitressing. In fact, there were many nights when she left her shift owing the bar money for all the alcohol she drank. I frequently was mad at my sister because of this. After all, we had tiny mouths to feed and bills to pay and we needed her paycheck as well as mine to make those things happen.

Plus Barbara often brought men home and was typically too hung over to wake up before noon. I wanted Barbara to take responsibility for her son, but every morning Travis began crying from her room and I ended up going in to get him so I could care for him for the day. My job at McDonald's became a thing of the past.

To make up for the furniture we had to leave in Anderson, Barbara and I had rented some pieces from a nearby Rent-a-Center. Our bill was $70 a week, and before long we couldn't pay. I remember hiding under the couch when their bill collectors came banging on the door looking for their money. What could I say? We didn't have it.

I also was very conflicted about my role in life during this time. I was just beginning to realize all I was missing by being a teen mom. I didn't get to go on dates or have sleepover parties with girlfriends. I didn't get to be that giggly teen girl who whispers secrets to her friend as they walk down the hallway at school or fill out college applications and hold my breath while I hoped for good news. Instead I was a destitute mom, but I also desperately wanted to be the kid I still was. It seemed that the only time I fit in with kids my age was with other drug users, or on the rare occasions when Barbara brought the party home with her and I mingled.

On top of this, I was still taking prescribed medications to balance my moods. I had been taking Trazodone since I was twelve, but more recently other antianxiety and antidepressant medications had been added. I felt like I had been taking prescription medicines all my life. Uppers, downers, anything the doctors could find to balance my mood or energy they prescribed for me, and all of it ended up messing with my head more than it helped. I was also mixing cocaine, street pills, alcohol, Ecstasy, and mushrooms— anything to make me feel better and relieve the overwhelming stress of responsibility. I am embarrassed to say that any money left over after we paid for rent, food, and diapers was spent on cigarettes, alcohol, and drugs.

One day I snapped. Barbara was with the kids at home one evening when I went to a party. There was an array of drugs there—as there were at most of the parties I went to. We never went to a party to celebrate anything or anyone, or even really to visit with one another. The main purpose of the parties I went to was to get high.

As things began to wind down I found that I didn't want to go home, so I hitchhiked to a party that I knew was going on in another town. Once I got there I got into a fight with an older guy I barely knew and for a reason I no longer remember he slapped me hard across the face. I started to hitchhike home but ended up getting into a car going the other way and wound up far away from Barbara, Abbie, and Travis—and I still didn't want to go back.

I called a friend, a guy I had met at bluegrass festival who I knew partied like I did. He gave me directions to his house out in the country, an older two-story house with rickety steps. I stayed there for three days thinking about my life, and those three days were the only days I ever thought about giving Abbie up. I thought about that a lot during those hours. While I was still drunk and high I called my mother and told her I couldn't handle being a parent. I don't remember what she said to me but I do know that after I sobered up I went home and was very glad I did.

My lovely daughter really was, and is, everything to me. It was only the dangerous combination of drugs, alcohol, stress, and being overwhelmed financially and emotionally that made me doubt my ability to parent her. I am so humiliated about this time in my life, and am very glad Abbie was too young to remember it.

Thirteen

★

Legal Troubles

Growing up in today's society is so difficult. I hear horror stories from other moms about their daughters getting pregnant and doing drugs, and this is one of my biggest fears when it comes to my daughters. Recently, I went on a school field trip with Abbie and I was shocked to see the contrast between Abbie and the other girls in her class. Even more shocking, however, was the contrast in age between the other fifth-grade moms and me. Here I was, twenty-five years old, standing next to women who were mostly in their late thirties or early forties. It was a bit intimidating to say the least.

My age is something that I knew was going to be an issue one day. "Abbie, your mom is so young," one of the girls said as we all stood in line. Abbie just looked at me and smiled. She knows without a doubt that I love her. Then Abbie giggled and said, "I know." I have never lied to her. I have told her that I was a young teenager when she was born. I also told her that I missed out on so much, but I wouldn't change a single day of it because she is one of the greatest things to happen to me. Abbie knows that the struggles I went through is not the life that I want for her. Being a teen mother is not easy, but that's the thing about being a parent at any age. It's a hard job and all you can do is your best.

Abbie is ten, and is at an age when her horizons are rapidly expanding. One purpose of community service, middle school dances, church socials, and the like is to give kids the opportunity to explore relationships with the opposite sex while adults look on. If any relationship hints of the inappropriate, or if parents do not approve of the person their son or daughter sets their sights on, the teen is gently redirected. I never had that guidance, and it affects me in relationships to this day. I am just now learning to take things slow, and to consider before moving ahead. Instead of a date for the sophomore spring fling, I had a baby to look after.

However, even though I was way too young, I loved being a mom. I loved looking into my daughter's eyes and seeing her smile. I also loved snuggling with her, loving her, and taking care of her. Abbie especially loved it when I played hand games with her and we laughed and laughed. She really was such a smart baby.

We had always had pets when I was growing up, and I had become pretty adept at training them. When it came time to teach

Abbie, I approached the same concepts with her that I used to teach my pets to sit, stay, and come. I really didn't have anything else to draw from, but you know what? It worked just fine. This was also during a time when Disney and other channels, such as PBS, had a lot of educational television for young kids, and Abbie watched many episodes of those kinds of shows.

But as any single parent knows, being a mom or dad is exceptionally hard when there is only one of you. On top of my youth and lack of financial resources, another part of my difficulty in caring for Abbie was that her father had been jailed for molestation of a minor: me.

When I was still pregnant with Abbie I had to appear in front of a grand jury and testify about my relationship with Brendan. I was positive that I could convince the members of the jury that we were in love, and that that fact would make a difference. The truth was, in spite of all the adult attempts to keep us away from each other, we were still a couple. Brendan was not allowed in the hospital for Abbie's birth, nor was he there when any of my family or friends were around, but he did sneak in to see us when no one else was there.

Brendan also drove me from Anderson to Fairbanks for my grand jury appearance. The grand jury met in a huge building with lots of balconies. It was probably a courthouse of some sort, but it was really intimidating to a young girl like me. After I walked through the metal detectors I was led down a long hallway and instructed to sit outside the grand jury room in a chair where

I stayed for a long time. When they were ready for me the door opened and I walked in.

I think there are only twelve people on a grand jury, but it seemed to me that there was a sea of about eighty faces. Everyone was seated at a huge, round table, and there was a thirteenth seat with a microphone in front of it for me.

It felt like the questioning went on for hours, but it probably was only ten to fifteen minutes. I remember seeing the eyes of every member of the grand jury boring into me, but I can't remember a single face. They asked a lot of questions along the lines of how Brendan and I met, if I knew how old he was, if he knew how old I was, where we had sex, and how often. I told them that the number of times we were together was easily a hundred times or more; that Brendan and I had been a couple for several years and that that was what couples did. Brendan had encouraged me to be honest, and I was. Then I added, "You are taking away the only person who will help me. He is the only stable person I have in my life." And that was the truth.

Later, after Abbie was born, a trooper came to my house and swabbed the inside of her cheek. The result of that swab proved that Brendan was indeed Abbie's father. This meant that Brendan had to go to court, and I was frightened that he would do jail time. Even though we were not living in the same house and could not be together publicly, in my mind we were a family.

Brendan had a habit of drinking Bacardi and Coke. When we sat down in the courtroom for his hearing he swirled a sixteen-ounce bottle of Coke in a familiar manner that made me suspect that he may have added a load of rum to it. Brendan pled guilty, and because of that instead of one hundred counts of sexual molestation of a minor, the charges were dropped to two: the first time we were intimate and the time I got pregnant.

I was devastated. He was sentenced to fifteen months, but ended up serving just under twelve, as he was released early for good behavior.

I understood the reason for laws like the one used to convict Brendan, but I found the decision difficult to accept because Brendan was the only one who provided me with stability and normalcy during that time. I definitely believed there should be laws to protect minors from predators, but in this instance the illicit relationship I had with Brendan was my only safety net. It was another huge source of conflict for me, and to be honest I'm not sure I have completely worked through it yet.

It should have been a simple thing. A twenty-three-year old man had relations with a thirteen-year-old girl. He should not have done that. He should not have taken advantage of my youth and inexperience in the ways of life. Even though I had seen and done a lot more than I should have in my thirteen years, I was still the vulnerable one. I was still a child.

On the other hand, Brendan provided me with more solidity than anyone else at the time. He was my rock, my sounding board, and we really did love each other. Why else would he have agreed to that crazy plan of my mother's that would have shipped us off to

Alabama to get married? He didn't have to agree to it, and there was no good incentive in it for him other than his feelings for me.

★

With Brendan in jail, I felt totally alone. In my conflict, I didn't understand why Brendan could not be there to wake up with the baby in the middle of the night or help me with other areas of child care. I didn't understand why he couldn't console me after a bad day or why we couldn't spend time together as other couples did.

Plus when you are fifteen a year is a really long time. Brendan wrote us several letters and sent a birthday card to Abbie for her first birthday, but this was so not the life I had envisioned for us as a family. Brendan and I had an understanding that whenever he got through with whatever punishment he was given we would be together. That was all that mattered to me, and that's why it was so important to Brendan that we tell the truth whenever we were questioned about our relationship. He didn't want the authorities to come back on him with something new. He wanted it all out in the open and dealt with as quickly as possible.

I can see now that my confusion led directly back to the extreme dysfunction of the people in my life, family and friends alike. I had never known normalcy. Instead, this craziness was all I knew, and the ways of regular people didn't make sense to me. At all.

Needing comfort, I reverted to the behavior I had learned from other women in my life and began seeing a new boyfriend, whom

I'll call Allen. Allen was the boy I had lost my virginity to and was the total opposite of Brendan in both appearance and personality. Where Brendan was comfortable and fun, Allen and I were like fire together. My time with him was exhilarating.

Allen also was married, and I find it interesting now that I didn't see his marriage as a problem in us being together. It was totally wrong, but here again, Allen was older. Not as old as Brendan was, but Allen was in his twenties. Marriage is a sacred commitment before God, and neither of us was honoring his commitment to that. Then again, my self-esteem was so low, and I was so needy that I was thrilled by any attention an older boy or man gave me. Besides, the adults in my life had regularly slept with married people, or they had been married when they slept with other people, so I didn't understand the seriousness.

One day Allen and I were in a trailer his mother had purchased a few days before. Neighbors, believing the trailer where we were had been broken into, called the police.

When the police showed up they didn't believe us when we told them that Allen's mother owned the trailer, and things quickly got ugly. One officer snatched me by my hair, dragged me through the house, down a set of seven steps, and then kicked me in the ribs. If you've never had that happen to you I can tell you it hurts. A lot. He then proceeded to kick me in the face and beat me so brutally that my shoes came off.

To top it off, I was charged with resisting arrest, trespassing, and assault. When they shoved me into the police car someone handcuffed me, but I am not the daughter of the world's best bounty hunter for nothing. Early on I learned to remove any kind of handcuff put on my wrists, and I slipped this set off very easily.

I was first taken to the hospital, as my injuries were that severe. Then I was taken to juvenile court, but rather than stay in jail, I was released to the Family Focus program in Fairbanks. This program has since closed but was a shelter for runaway, throwaway, and homeless kids.

Despite my initial reluctance about being in the shelter, I loved it there. We had three good, hot meals every day, and the staff led classes in life skills that I found very helpful. It was the most structured environment I had been in in many years.

The program was centered around a huge house on Cushman Street with a welcoming front porch. Upstairs there were several large bedrooms, with boys rooming on one side of the house and girls on the other. Each bedroom had four to six bunk beds. I had never had the opportunity to go to camp, or even go to or have sleepovers with friends when I was growing up. This was my opportunity to catch up on those missed experiences. The other girls and I stayed up every night talking and talking. It was so much fun. One girl even gave me a pair of shorts that I have to this day. I keep them as a reminder of that stable time in my life.

One day during our free hour I went across the street to the park with another girl who lived in the house. We each found a swing, and as I toed the gravel under my feet we began to talk. Her problems, I found, were far more normal than mine. She was a runaway who was having problems with her parents. I found myself really interested in her life and in her perspectives. I felt so free sitting there. I had no responsibilities other than to get back to the house in time for dinner. It was the first time I had ever experienced that kind of freedom.

The problems of that girl were typical of most of the people in the house. While the other girls were worrying about their friends and school, I was worrying about diapers and rent. It was interesting for me to listen to their concerns and compare them to my own. And while I desperately missed Abbie, I enjoyed sleeping in and not having to worry about where my next meal was coming from. My concern over Abbie aside, it was a time of rest and no stress.

The place was very nice. Downstairs there was a game room and a TV room. We all had daily chores, and as long as we did them and followed the rules we were allowed several hours of free time every day. If anyone broke the rules, however, they were asked to leave . . . and they could not come back. In my case that meant I would have to go to juvenile jail, so I was sure to do everything asked of me.

After I settled in I saw a probation officer, and he was so concerned with the extent of my beating that he got all the charges against me dropped. I thought I'd be free to go after that but for some reason I had to stay. It might have been because the people there knew I had nowhere else to go that officials thought was suitable for Abbie and me. My mother had also told the people that she did not want me to stay with her or in her house. The news that I had to remain at the group home did not sit well with me, mostly because I was frantic with worry. I had just learned that temporary custody of Abbie had been given to my mother.

I loved my mother, but the reality was that there was no way she could safely care for a young toddler. Plus, right after Travis was born she chose to move in with her boyfriend who lived ninety miles away, rather than stay at home with her pregnant daughter and week-old grandson. That said a lot to me about my mother's interest in being a grandmother. I pleaded with everyone I could and finally convinced them of the seriousness of the situation in which they had placed my daughter.

Words cannot describe how happy and relieved I was when Abbie was brought back to me. I think the best way to convey my emotions was that with Abbie in my arms I felt complete. I never wanted to let her out of my sight again.

I knew that Family Focus had made a unique exception in bringing Abbie in. Normally young children were not allowed. In fact, I think I was the first teen mom in the home. To accommodate Abbie, and still keep as many of their rules as they could, they put Abbie and me in a special room downstairs. That was fine, except that we had to stay in that room or in the game room. Plus they would not allow me to put up a baby gate to either room, as a gate was deemed a fire hazard. Abbie was both walking and running by this time, and it was next to impossible to keep an active little girl like her confined to such small spaces.

She was used to having the run of the house she lived in and didn't understand why she had to stay in those two rooms. It was a frustrating time for everyone.

In addition, the Family Focus staff was interested to see that Abbie was well cared for and took time to assess my ability as a parent. Somehow that meant they forbade me to discipline my daughter. Not that I was a cruel or inhumane parent by any means, but toddlers need boundaries. Toddlers keep busy exploring their world, and if they are not admonished from time to time can get hurt. I have known some toddlers who like to climb shelves, or squeeze under low beds. Both of those activities can be quite harmful if the child is not corrected, and Family Focus did not allow me to do that.

Before my beating, Abbie and I had loved watching the new movie *Finding Nemo*. We also loved the Wiggles series and television episodes of *SpongeBob SquarePants*. In fact, Abbie's first birthday party had a SpongeBob theme. After the party my mother offered me my first experience with meth, but that is another story altogether. Now, at Family Focus, we were even prohibited from watching the shows that Abbie loved.

For the second time in as many weeks, and for entirely different reasons, I became frantic about Abbie's well-being. Fortunately, Allen called not too many days later to tell the staff that he had arranged for me to stay with Jimmy. The organization felt that with Jimmy I would be under the proper care and supervision of an adult, and released me. I was checked on for a time, but not too closely. After Abbie and I had been at Jimmy's for a short while, we moved back into Barbara's Section 8 housing.

★

While the entire experience was traumatic on many fronts, after I was released from the shelter I came to a new realization. It was the first time in my life that it struck me in a clear and present manner that I might be heading down the wrong path. That probably was an obvious observation to everyone else, but it was an eye-opening realization for me. I don't know if it was the three square meals a day, the life skills classes, the conversations with my bunkmates, or my ongoing fear for Abbie's safety, but something inside me said "enough."

While it's true that normalcy is an entirely foreign concept when all you know is dysfunction, one day the sixteen-year-old me looked at my mess of a life and knew that a better way of living had to be out there. I longed to go back to the safety of my special tree in Hawai'i where I had done all my television "shows" and in the sanctity of its comforting branches ask God where the life I dreamed about was. Where were all the wonderful things I envisioned when I used to ride my bike around town?

I remembered many of the Bible stories that Dad had read to us, and I remembered many of Pastor Jeremiah's sermons. In those stories were truth and promise, and I badly needed both of those things in my life. I also had a daughter and wondered what role

God would play in her life. I remembered my churchgoing days and wondered if my child would be God-loving.

Even though I was questioning God and His role in Abbie's—and in my—life, I wasn't yet ready to follow His plan for me, or even seek it out. I didn't know what or how or where, but I knew without a doubt that I had to do something big that would permanently change things for the better. I didn't get there right away, but change was on my radar and would soon make its presence known. But first I had to hit rock bottom.

Fourteen

★

Swallowing My Pride

*A*s *an adult I* understand that even though your heart wants something it is not necessarily the best thing for you. Brendan is a prime example of this. I rationalized every part of our relationship to make it seem right. When Brendan was in prison, he snuck letters to me. A mutual friend was our go-between and gave the envelopes to me. Brendan even sent Abbie a birthday card. I turned these rare bits of communication into proof of Brendan being a responsible father.

In another instance, Brendan told me his job was to detail cars. I took this to mean he painted fancy designs on the vehicles when in reality Brendan cleaned car interiors. I so wanted Brendan to be in Abbie's life that I let my heart take over any bit of common sense that I had. In fact, as Brendan's release neared, he became all I could think about. Brendan, Abbie, and I could finally be a family!

Abbie was just over sixteen months old when Brendan became a free man. By this time she had grown into a happy little girl who loved playing with her cousin Travis. She never got upset when he took away the toy she was playing with. She was so patient with him then, and still is today.

To his credit, Brendan was clean and sober when he was released. He even bathed regularly, something he had not done before. I have since learned that not bathing can be signs of either mental illness or addiction.

I, too, had changed a lot during that long, long year. I had grown up in many ways, and it wasn't so easy for other people to take advantage of me now. I wasn't quite as confident in the abilities of others as I used to be, and I had even developed a little bit of self-esteem. That's why Barbara was just one of several people who were amazed that I had let Brendan back into my life. "Why?" she asked. "He causes so many problems for you. Why bother?"

The simple answer was that I loved Brendan. But it was more than that. He was Abbie's father, and I wanted her to have a dad. It was also the Svengali-like effect he had over me. I'd had Brendan in my life too long not to have him there, if that makes any sense. As Barbara would not allow Brendan in our house, even though he often brought us food and other necessities, Abbie and I moved with Brendan to a small room in a set of construction barracks.

The room was about the size of a bathroom. Really, I kid you not. The place was beyond tiny.

Construction barracks are set up as temporary housing for construction workers. Each "room" was stacked either on top of or next to another unit. The room provided shelter, but just barely. Our unit was reached after walking down a long center hall that had rooms on both the left and right. In the room was a double bed, and across from the bed was a bench with a microwave on top and a small refrigerator underneath. There was barely enough room to squeeze between the bed and the bench. A tiny window completed the room.

The transition was hard for me on several accounts. First, the Section 8 housing that Barbara had was roomy and nice, and it was difficult to get used to living in the small, dingy efficiency. Second, unbeknownst to Brendan, I was still seeing Allen, and Allen was quite upset that Brendan was back in my life. Although I was living with Brendan, several nights a week I stayed out all night with Allen. I wasn't sure whom I loved more. "Neither" should have been the easy answer to that problem, but I was not yet healthy enough emotionally to go that route.

The end result was that Allen moved to a place just two blocks from us. While I understand now how unfair I was being to both men and to myself, I was so engrossed in my own drama that I couldn't see how dysfunctional the entire situation was. Of course I should have stopped seeing Allen, because he was married. And

I should have stopped seeing Brendan because of the age difference and because he was a sex offender.

To complicate matters, my old boyfriend James Jenkins also lived within blocks of us. On a typical day I'd leave Brendan, go to McDonald's, and spend a dollar fifty on two double cheeseburgers. This was all I could afford to eat for the entire day. Then I'd often wave at James as he passed by in a car with his mother as I headed to Allen's. I couldn't choose between Brendan and Allen, but fortunately fate stepped in and forced me to decide.

Even though I tried to be secretive about where I was going and what I was doing, one day Brendan discovered the truth about Allen and me and made me choose. I found I didn't have to think long before I chose Brendan. I really still was in love with him. Shortly after that we moved in with Brendan's dad, Ken, because we had been kicked out of the tiny, crummy barracks we had been living in and had nowhere else to go.

★

With Brendan's dad able to take care of Abbie during the day, I lied about my age and got a job—or, I should say, lots of jobs. I moved from job to job roughly every two weeks. That's because most of my employers required me to take a drug test when they first hired me. By the time the results of the test came back it was roughly two weeks later. I knew I'd never pass the test, so I'd collect my one paycheck and move on. I was a housekeeper at about six different hotels and was at the Days Inn the longest because they didn't drug-test at all. I also had a job for a while at a great coffee shop on Cushman Street in Fairbanks called McCafferty's. I love coffee, so it was a great fit for me. Besides, McCafferty's is a very cool place. If you are ever in the area you should check it out.

One day I came home from work to find Abbie's private parts bright red. You can imagine my shock and outrage.

Abbie was about two, but not yet verbal enough to tell me what had happened. I had to know the truth, though, so Brendan and I took Abbie to the hospital. Once we got there they put Brendan in one room, me in another, and Abbie in a third room.

A thousand thoughts were going through my head as I sat in the room by myself and waited. I also knew that by taking Abbie to the hospital there was a possibility that Child Protective Services might step in. But I had no choice. Abbie was not old enough to tell us what happened, so I had to be her voice. I knew I had to do the responsible thing for my daughter, and this was it. If I lost her in the process, at least it was better losing her because I was trying to do the right thing than because someone thought I was not attentive enough as a mother.

When the doctor examined Abbie he found that her hymen had been broken, but he could not determine if she had been sexually molested. Sometimes a girl's hymen will break if she is active, and Abbie was certainly an active little girl, but I was told that usually happens when the girl is much older than Abbie was.

Oftentimes not knowing the truth is worse than knowing, and this was one of those times. How I wished I had a definitive answer about what happened to Abbie. I didn't know who to trust or who to believe, and that made me so confused I didn't know which way was up.

One or two mornings later I was awakened when two detectives in business suits pounded on our door. During my life I'd had a lot of law enforcement people bang on my door for one reason or another, but they were always in uniform. These were my first "suits," and they scared the crap out of me. The detectives asked me to show them where everyone in the house slept, so I first showed them Ken's couch in the living room. Then I took them into the one bedroom where Brendan, Abbie, and I slept.

One of the detectives then took me outside and started in on me. "What are you thinking?"

In short, they gave me twelve hours to pack my things and leave the house with Abbie, or my daughter would be removed from my care. The detectives were quite firm about this, and when they left I knew I had no other choice. The detectives were right; we needed to leave. I also know without a doubt that God stepped in and sent those detectives to my door to get us out of there. I shudder to think what might have happened to Abbie had we not left when we did.

The trouble was that I had nowhere to go. Barbara had moved in with a man who was actively doing hard drugs, so I couldn't go there. My mother and John had no room, and besides, they had made it clear that they didn't want Abbie and me.

My only option was to move into the old mint green Ford Focus that Brendan had given me. As I prepared to move I became very angry with Brendan. Here I was having to move into a *car* with our toddler daughter, and his attitude was "Oh, well." His lack of concern for the situation and "easy come, easy go" attitude should have let me know how deeply he was back into drugs, but my own drug use most likely masked that thought process for me.

★

I spent the next few weeks moving the car from place to place so as not to get caught by the police. I even drove from Fairbanks to Anderson and parked the car by the river there for a few days before I was chased out. On the way back to Fairbanks the car began acting funny and I was afraid we'd break down, but we didn't.

In Fairbanks, most businesses do not let people park in their lots overnight because they do not want "riffraff" around their storefronts. After searching long and hard, I finally found a safe enough place where a lot of homeless people parked. Then it hit me. I was one of these people.

I was homeless, too.

How had I gotten here? I wondered. The past few years had melted into a sea of memories, and while I tried to find the one reason why I was living in my car with my young daughter, I couldn't come up with it. Instead, the reasons were way too many and far too sad.

There was a third person living in the car with us, though, and that was our dog, Pepper. Brendan had come home with Pepper one day a few months back but I soon realized that he was not going to be responsible enough to take care of her, so I gladly stepped up. Pepper was a knee-high black-and-white mixed-breed dog. She could possibly have been some kind of Labrador/terrier cross, but it didn't matter to me what she was. I loved her, and her shaggy presence definitely made me feel safer at night when Abbie and I slept in the backseat of the car. Never have I underestimated the role Pepper played in keeping us safe during that terrible time.

By this time it was October and it was getting very cold in the evenings. I was so grateful to have Pepper in the car with us. I'd put her between Abbie and me when we settled in for the night, and the heat of her body kept us warm. That dog could really put out some heat. But I knew the nights would only get colder, and with no other options in sight, I broke down and called Dad's bonds office in Hawai'i.

I had wanted to call my dad for some time but didn't have Beth's number. To get Dad on the phone, everyone has to go through Beth first. I had hoped that either my dad or Beth would answer the line at Da Kine, my dad's bail bonds office, but instead I got another bondsman, Wesley.

Through Wesley I learned that Beth was having surgery soon and that Barbara was coming out to help with the kids while Beth recuperated. That was news to me, and honestly I didn't think it was going to happen. Barbara was so absorbed in her new boyfriend that I didn't believe anything short of a hurricane would pull her out of Alaska.

During the next few weeks my conversations with Wesley moved to discussion with Beth and then with Dad. I hadn't spoken to him in three years, and with the exception of my brief visit in Colorado when we went after the gang rapists, I hadn't seen him in more than six years.

I didn't know what to think when Dad said he wanted me to come to Hawai'i instead of Barbara, but I knew I was going to do it, even after Dad began listing my upcoming duties in a very businesslike manner. I know he wanted to be sure that I knew I was expected to work and contribute to the family if I was to live in the house with them.

You cannot imagine how grateful I was when Dad sent plane tickets for Abbie and me. I was really looking forward to a new life, a new start. I also badly wanted to meet my younger sister and brother, Bonnie Jo and Garry Boy. These two cuties had been born in 1998 and 2001, but even though it was now late fall of 2004, I had never laid eyes on them. I also couldn't wait to see Cecily again, and just be in Hawai'i where it was warm and the ocean could soothe me.

While I was excited about the trip, I was a little nervous about Dad and Beth meeting Abbie. This was because they had never supported my relationship with Brendan. I understand now why that was, but back then I was very angry with them about that, especially because at Christmas the year before, Dad and Beth had sent a ton of presents to Alaska for Barbara and Travis but none for Abbie or me. I'd like to think because Barbara and Travis had been back and forth so many times that Dad and Beth knew Barbara and Travis much better than they did Abbie and me. But I really think it was more along the lines of "look what you got yourself into and now you are stuck with the consequences."

The second reason I was nervous was that I had recently determined that, somehow, the perpetual cycle of dysfunction and abuse in our family was going to stop with me. All of the adults in my life had contributed to this where I was concerned—including Dad, Beth, my mother, and all of their combined spouses, boyfriends, and girlfriends. I was not going to allow any of that to trickle down to my daughter. I had seen normally functioning families on television and had gotten glimpses of them when I talked with other people. I realized, probably for the first time, that not everyone lived like we did. Not everyone drank or did drugs. There was an entire world out there full of people who didn't constantly fight, who instead talked through their problems and made positive changes. There were even families who stayed together.

I realized I was a mess and knew I had a long, hard climb in front of me. However, I was done with the way I was living. I was done being around people whose only response to stress was to get high. I was absolutely done with abuse. I didn't know how I was going to stop this vicious cycle, but I definitely knew I was going to do it.

Since leaving Brendan I had not been drinking at all and my drug use was (almost) down to nothing. I was trying so hard to change and I knew that meant I had to stay away from people who used—people such as Barbara, Brendan, and Allen. I wanted to change for Abbie, but I also wanted to change for myself. In fact, this was the first time I had ever tried to do anything positive for me. It was hard, and I was scared that I would never succeed. So scared in fact that I put too much pressure on myself and partied way too hard every day during the short week before I left for Hawai'i. I knew that once I got there my cocoon of isolation would end. Could I stay sober with other people around? Could I not use when I was accountable to people other than myself? I'd find out soon enough. In Hawai'i I'd have to adhere to Beth's house rules, and that meant no drinking or drugs whatsoever.

Fifteen

★

The Reality of Reality Television

I had lived with drugs as part of my life for so long that it was terrifying to me to live without them. Even though I have been drug-free for a number of years now, my body was so addicted that I know I have to be watchful so as not to slide back into that lifestyle in the future. It's like a smoker starting to smoke again after twenty years, only it's a thousand times worse.

I have found that there is a very fine line between using drugs and not using drugs. Some of the people whom I have met in AA make their entire lives about not being high. This was the other end of the pendulum swing from my former friends who took drugs. Their entire lives were all about getting high. I knew I wanted to live a fuller, richer life, but that often is hard.

My biggest craving now is to pop a pill when I can't sleep, am stressed, or don't feel well. After all, isn't that what we are told to do in advertisements? In commercials? And it seems to me that many doctors these days do nothing more than write prescriptions for pills. I have been medicated since before I was a teenager, so I learned early on that the solution to a problem was a pill. I have had to unlearn all of that.

About a year ago I realized that when I was stressed my cravings intensified, so I took steps to reduce my interactions with stressful people and stressful situations. It took months, but I am now in a place where I am far less stressed than I used to be. Last week I went out with friends who were drinking. Not that I intentionally sought out friends who drink, but it is hard to find people my age who don't. That night I drank my iced tea all evening and had a great time, which meant I had no temptation. Today I know my triggers and I have the tools I need to not use, but it wasn't always that way.

Before I left for Hawai'i, a "friend" gave me a gram of meth. I knew I couldn't smoke it in the air, so I chopped it up and snorted as much of it as I could on the plane. That meant I had to leave Abbie in her seat while I went to partake in the bathroom. What kind of mother does that? I can see now that while I truly wanted a different way of life, I was not yet ready to do all the work that entailed.

Upon my arrival in Honolulu, I was amazed at the height of the buildings and the size of the city. In Fairbanks they have a limit of roughly seven stories on the buildings due to the tundra there.

In Honolulu more than a dozen of the hotels were forty stories or taller. Currently there are more than 470 high-rise buildings in Honolulu, and the city ranks fourth in the nation for these towering structures. Only New York City, Chicago, and Los Angeles have more tall buildings. It was total culture shock. I couldn't fathom that there were so many places for people to live. Then I realized that it had been about nine years since I had been in Hawai'i and even longer than that since I had been in Honolulu. Compared to Anderson and Fairbanks, the many tall buildings were a huge sensory overload. It didn't help that I was as high as a kite.

I vaguely knew that my dad had a television show, but I didn't understand what being on national—or international—television meant. Earlier that year Barbara and I had watched one or maybe two episodes of the first season of Dad's show. Neither of us really understood the concept. You have to remember that this was back when reality shows were brand-new and not everyone knew what they were.

My dad had ordered a limousine taxi for me, and when I arrived at his modest ranch house I was even more astonished to find a *Dog the Bounty Hunter* video camera stuck in my face as I tried to get out of the vehicle. Abbie and I walked to the door, and I was a little surprised that Dad was there to greet me. He had sounded so businesslike over the phone I wasn't sure if he was going to be glad to see me. But his big Dad hug let me know how he really felt.

Our reunion aired on the first episode of the show's second season. It is titled "Baby's Back in Town," and discerning viewers will notice that my eyes are fully dilated. I watched the show again recently and was shocked at my dirty, stringy hair and the horrible dark eye shadow I wore. Even worse, a lot of what people said to me seemed to go right over the top of my head. I could see that I was desperately trying to get up to speed on all that was happening, and failing miserably.

Back then, however, I thought no one would notice that I was high. I also thought I looked a lot cooler than I really did. That's drugs for you. They completely distort reality.

After my arrival had been filmed, we all sat down to eat. If you have never been to Hawai'i, it really is a long way from anywhere. Flying from Fairbanks to Anchorage to Honolulu takes the better part of a full day, and both Abbie and I were exhausted. But instead of resting I realized I was supposed to make conversation at the table. I did my best to hold up my end of the discussion, but I was so clueless. Later, when we'd go out to eat, I didn't recognize a thing on the menu. I always looked for a cheeseburger because it was the only item I was familiar with. Once, Dad gave me a $100 bill. I held on to it for about a month because I didn't know what to spend it on. It had been a long time since I'd seen that much money.

On that first day everyone asked how it felt to be back with my dad. I really didn't know. I had been there only an hour or so and hadn't had a chance to talk to him much. I did get a chance to meet Bonnie Jo and Garry Boy, though, and found them to be very sweet at first.

The Reality of Reality Television

After lunch Beth had a follow-up doctor's appointment from her surgery, so she and Dad got in the car and drove off. They left me with Garry Boy and Bonnie Jo, and Beth's daughter, Cecily, whom I hadn't seen in many years. Garry must have been about three, Bonnie about six, and Cecily around eleven years of age.

Garry Boy immediately punched me in the face, Bonnie Jo got out her pet gecko, and Cecily turned up her rap music so loud they could probably hear it all the way over on the Big Island. The day deteriorated from there. I was so overwhelmed and frustrated that I wanted to cry. Today I have great relationships with these kids and I love them with all my heart. But back then they tested me every time I turned around.

The first few weeks I was there I tried my best to settle in. I felt so out of my element with the "sophisticated" production people who were always around and I didn't have any idea what I should say to them. Thinking back, these were probably the first "regular" people I had ever gotten to know. Everyone else in my life was completely dysfunctional, as were each of their relationships. I didn't have a clue how to relate to these kind, hardworking, normal people who surrounded us every waking moment of every day with cameras, microphones, and sound equipment.

The first two weeks I was in Hawai'i I spent a lot of time listening to Dad and Beth fight about what my place in the household should be. Both were concerned that I wasn't "doing anything," but other than Dad's very general list of tasks that he had talked to me about over the phone before I arrived, no one had told me what I should be doing. Plus I was way too overwhelmed with the show, the cultural differences, all the new people in my life, and (sometimes) trying to stay clean, to seek out responsibilities on my own.

Eventually it was decided that I should take care of the kids, and that's how I started getting Cecily, Bonnie Jo, Garry Boy, and Abbie up in the morning. I made sure they were washed and dressed and had eaten a good breakfast before I drove the older kids to school. Then I picked them up after school, drove them to any appointments, and made sure they did their homework. This is something I still do, every day, and I love it and those kids more than I can say. I could be very happy being the "Chapman nanny" forever.

Ironically, on my trips to and from the school I had to drive by Kalani High School. I was still just seventeen and should have been going to school myself. If I had been, that was the school I would have attended. Every day I thought of all the high school rituals I had missed and of the education I didn't get, and it made me sad.

In addition to caring for the kids, I also did most of the shopping. I'd line up all the kids by age and make them hold hands as we traipsed through the store, just as Dad had done with my siblings and me when we were small. I got a lot of stares from other shoppers that looked like they were wondering how I had so many kids while I was still so young. If they only knew!

It wasn't all work, though, and I soon made some friends through a woman named Tayshea who worked at Da Kine. You can see her on some of the show's early seasons. I also met other people, and unlike all the other groups of friends in my life most of these people were sober. In fact, the vast majority of them went to daily AA (Alcoholics Anonymous) meetings.

I was familiar with the concept of AA, but in Hawai'i I learned it is a culture unto itself. AA there is filled with a lot of great people who support one another in their sobriety journey, and I later found that the big AA handbook could have been written for and about me, I was that much of a classic addict. Even though in theory I was "trying" to stay away from drugs, I still thought constantly about getting high. Those of you who have struggled with any kind of addiction (whether it be drugs, alcohol, gambling, sex, or any other unhealthy obsession) know that even though you want to change, your brain and body often conspire against you. Some days getting high was all I could think about. Other days getting high was what I did.

When I first met my new friends I thought, great, I can get high with them. Surely one of them will slip. I watched this group very carefully for weeks, hoping to spot that one person who would slip so I could use with him or her. But I was surprised at the reaction when I approached several select individuals. "No, we won't use with you, but we *will* help you stay sober," they all said. Wow. I don't think anyone in my life had ever said no when I approached them about doing drugs. Hawai'i was proving to be a far bigger cultural change than I had ever imagined. Some of my AA friends began to build a *Dog the Bounty Hunter* float for Waiminala's upcoming Christmas parade. This was another thing I had trouble getting used to. In my druggie world back in Alaska people were really out for themselves. It was all about who could score the most drugs and who would share them with you. Here, people wanted to help you just for the sake of helping. There were no expectations in return. It took me a long time to understand and accept that kind of thinking.

In spring of the next year, 2005, Dad and Beth went to Las Vegas for a bail bonds convention. I took that opportunity to get high. The next morning Cecily, who was maybe twelve, was being as bratty as only a tween girl can. Still high, I did not have the emotional capability to deal with her attitude, and when she started to mouth off to me I slapped her across her face. It was absolutely an immature and wrong thing to do, but I was still just a kid myself. Even the best of teenage girls make a lot of errors. Plus I have no doubt that my brain had sucked up every ounce of drug that I had done the previous day. The old saying that you can't reason with someone who is drunk or high is very true. Their brains are not functioning at normal levels.

Cecily called Beth, and while I knew she was going to be mad, I was unprepared for the depth of her anger. "If you put a hand on my daughter again I'll kill you" was what I heard on the phone between Hawai'i and Vegas. I know that people often say things they don't mean, but right then I believed Beth with everything I had.

As soon as Cecily had hung up and I had dropped the kids off at school, I called Brendan. I couldn't do it anymore. The call to drugs was too strong, and I knew I had to leave Hawai'i. Brendan got me a ticket, and before I knew it, Abbie and I were back on a plane.

This time we had about a six-hour layover in Seattle. On the flight there I met a lady who had gone to Hawai'i to get clean. Her rehab hadn't done her a lot of good, as she couldn't wait to get home so she could use again. That's the thing about drugs. Your body and mind are so addicted that a twenty-eight- or thirty-day program often doesn't work. It took you a lot longer than that to build up your addiction, and it is going to take a lot longer than a month to kick it. That's why a lot of people need to go to rehab several times before it sticks.

I was so anxious to get some kind of drug in my body that I asked if I could go home with her. Forget the rest of the flight to Alaska; I just wanted to get high. To my surprise, she said sure, and after she got her baggage she said she'd get her car and swing back around the airport to get me. I half expected her not to show up, but a few minutes later, there she was. We went to her house and got high.

There is an unspoken bond between drug users. Even if they just met, there is instant camaraderie, instant friendship. Everyone feels loved. There are few boundaries and definitely no shame. At my new friend's house I found I wanted to forget all my troubles and stay right there in Seattle. I thought really hard about not getting back on the plane, but something inside me knew I had to get back to Alaska, so in plenty of time, the lady drove me back to the airport.

Brendan was the one who picked me up in Fairbanks. I had a huge bag filled with clothes, as Beth had bought me some nice things when I was in Hawai'i. I appreciated it, especially as I had arrived with next to nothing. As soon as Brendan had put my bag in the car, however, I picked a fight with him. I now realize that the fight was a product of poor judgment that resulted from the side effects of drugs, but back then, all I knew was that Brendan had irritated me beyond any tolerance I had. I just wanted to get back, go see my sister, and get high.

Sixteen

★

Hitting Rock Bottom

Life is so much simpler since I have gotten off drugs, and today my best friend when it comes to staying sober is God. One weekend more than a year ago when my girls were with Bo, I felt lonely. I began to read verses in the Bible. Then I really thought about the verses and I prayed. I felt a huge weight lift off my shoulders and today I know that I have God on my side all the time. I also know that I do not want to disappoint Him.

Getting to this point was not an easy process. Often when addicts fall, they fall hard. That's what happened to me. Looking back, I shouldn't have been surprised. Other than my new Hawai'ian friends who were in AA I had little support. I wasn't seeing a counselor and didn't attend any group sessions, read any helpful books, go to church, or have any sort of sponsor or mentor. I didn't even go to any AA or Narcotics Anonymous (NA) meetings. I'm not sure why that was other than I was so busy taking care of all the kids that there was no time.

Even if those things had been in place, however, there were no guarantees. Kicking a habit is tough. A 2007 Columbia University survey study of high school and middle school children (twelve studies over thirteen years) found that as a result of drug abuse, a teen struggles with unmanageable physical and emotional consequences compared to an adult addict. Furthermore, it was documented that children of substance-abusing parents have an increased risk of developing substance abuse issues, due to both genetics and environmental factors. The brain of an adolescent is not fully developed and is vulnerable to the alterations produced by drugs and alcohol. Plus issues related to adolescents and brain development can cause future psychological and physiological changes.

The odds for a successful recovery were definitely not in my favor.

When I think back I am amazed at all the encouragement I had from adults to use drugs. From the many adults I knew who didn't actively discourage my drug use, to people such as my mother who gave me drugs, there was never a time when someone sat me down and said that using was not a good idea. In addition, I never had anyone who showed me by their actions that a better way of life could be had without drugs than with. It's pretty sad when you think about it.

I remember when Barbara left Alaska the first time she was pregnant. She had gone to Colorado to get an abortion, and I was devastated by her absence. I missed her so much! My mother was the one who handed me a joint and said, "Here. This will make you feel better." My mother had first given me pot when I was twelve, and I actively began smoking it with her when I was just thirteen. She also used to leave us lines of cocaine in the bathroom as "presents." Other people have good family times with their mother at picnics, movies, or restaurants. Barbara and I got our bonding time with our mother doing drugs together in the living room.

As an adult I can see how very, very wrong all of this was, but at the time, I thought it was cool. Now when I talk to my mother all I talk to her about is the weather. I have so much anger that I don't want to bring up any topic that will spark an argument. This includes most topics, including family memories, lifestyles, politics, religion—you name it. I also make a point never to talk to her after six in the evening, as she is typically too drunk to make any sense.

★

Back in Fairbanks I wasn't thinking of any of this. I just needed a place to stay. Because I was under eighteen I could not "officially" sign a rental agreement, so I lied about my age when I met a guy who agreed to rent an apartment on Cushman and Lathrop Streets to me. Barbara had long been kicked out of the Section 8 housing program for not following the rules, and she and Travis moved in a day or so later.

After we got settled I remained high most of the time. I am now so ashamed that I traded sex for drugs as often as four nights a week. One meth dealer was a particularly disgusting guy. After I let him use my body he always left me some meth. But I preferred cocaine, so I called another friend and traded. I was so lost.

One time I had a house full of people. We were all partying when a domestic dispute arose next door. It must have been a slow night in Fairbanks because before we knew it there were five or six police cars within spitting distance of my front door. We all hit the floor and hid there for some time. At other times I was so high that I remember crawling around on the floor because I was convinced the police were outside my door when they weren't.

I lived in a basement apartment. When I was standing, my head was on the same level as the ground outside. All I could see out the window were people's feet. When I was high, I prayed that no one would come to my door. On days when I was sober, I opened my door wide to show the world that my apartment was clean, that I had food, and that I was as normal as anyone else.

I'd like to tell you what Abbie liked to do at this stage of her development, but unfortunately my memories of this time are foggy. My mother, Barbara, and I were getting high every day. Even if we were not buying drugs, they were being supplied. All I remember is that I wanted to sleep but never wanted to eat, cook, or clean. I am so disgusted by my behavior that of all the times for someone to take my child away, this would have been it.

Instead of my Hawai'ian AA friends, in Alaska I began hanging with a group of Hell's Angels. I had known a lot of the people in the group since I was twelve, so this was nothing new. In the Hell's Angels culture, women are mostly classified as either daughters or whores. The guys protected the daughters, and as daughters, Barbara and I had fallen under their protective arm several times.

One night after I had been back in Alaska for several weeks, Barbara went to the airport with a Hell's Angel to pick up a friend. She left at about 10:00 p.m., and at 3:00 a.m. I woke up to find another Hell's Angel at the foot of my bed. Apparently Barbara had been arrested and needed my help.

A few months earlier Barbara had begun dating a guy who was in the military. This was a guy who was head over heels in love with her. Because he loved her so much, one day he gave her a credit card with a $10,000 limit. Of course, Barbara maxed out the card in no time, buying things such as a camera, food, and clothing. Whatever she or I wanted, we bought. But when the credit card company began calling him for payment, he claimed Barbara had stolen the card.

I later learned that at the airport before the friend's flight came in, Barbara had been quite loud. Security came over and asked to see her identification, and when they ran a check on it they found she was wanted for theft of the credit card. Long story short, the

Hell's Angel had woken me to see if I could help Barbara with the $1,500 bond needed for her bail.

We had nowhere near that amount of money. I don't think I could have helped her if her bail was $150. Not knowing what else to do, I stayed up all night to call friends to ask for $10 here, $15 there, in hopes that together we could raise enough money that Barbara could be released. When I reached the end of our list of friends I had pulled a lot of the money together, but we were still a long way from the amount needed.

When Barbara finally called from jail, she was hysterical. She wanted out now and said it was up to me—almost like it was my fault she was there. Another issue with her release was that we couldn't find a bondsman in Fairbanks, and the only ones I could find in Anchorage didn't want to fool with a bond that small. I began to panic, as I wasn't sure I could ever get Barbara out of jail. By this time it was March and our kids were just a few months shy of three years old. Travis kept asking where his mother was and I didn't have a clue what to tell him.

Then a miracle happened. Barbara's tax refund arrived, and along with the other money I had gathered, it was enough to release her from jail. But first I had to find a way to cash the check. Barbara and I looked enough alike that I risked my own freedom to secure hers. I took her driver's license and the check to a Fred Meyer store and pretended to be Barbara as the clerk exchanged the check for cash. I was so nervous I could hardly breathe, and when the cash was handed to me I resisted the impulse to run as fast as I could out the front door. I was relieved to have Barbara out of jail, but more than a little put out at my illegal involvement in the process.

A few days later my episode of *Dog the Bounty Hunter* aired. I might have missed it, but because the episode was the first one of the second season, A&E really hyped it, and everyone in Fairbanks knew I was going to be featured. When I turned on the television that evening at my mother's, I didn't know what to expect, and I almost didn't recognize the spaced-out girl on the show as me.

How could I look like that? I wondered. In my drugged-up state I saw myself as hip, together, and cool, but my TV image showed none of that. Was that how others saw me? Really? I had a hard time accepting that this was who I had become. People say a picture is worth a thousand words, and seeing my image on international television certainly was a shocking eye-opener for me. This was not who I wanted to be. Not at all. This was not anything close to the life I wanted for myself—or Abbie. I knew I'd had a good start during the few months I was in Hawai'i. Maybe, I thought, I could go back and build on that.

I had been in Alaska for only six weeks, but I had had enough. These past weeks had by far topped other times in my life as the worst ever. I had taken the drinking and drugging to new heights and could see that they were getting me nowhere. Plus I had risked a lot to forge Barbara's name on her tax refund and did not ever want to be in that kind of situation again.

For the first time I wondered what would happen to Abbie if I ever landed in jail. Who would take care of her? Nurture her?

Educate her? Keep her safe? Those were my jobs, and I realized I had found the motivation that would put my life on a much better track.

I called Dad, and in spite of everything he willingly took me back into his home. I am so grateful to him for that, especially because I understand that he could just as easily have said no. In response, I vowed to return to Hawai'i with a new mind-set. And I did. On April 8, 2005, Abbie, Travis, and I boarded a plane, and I have not been back to Alaska since. Barbara wanted to come, too, but the pending court date from her theft charge kept her in Alaska.

I loved Travis like my own son and wanted him to be part of the new life I was going to forge for Abbie and myself. The plan was for Barbara to head south after her legal troubles were over, but that didn't happen. More boyfriends, more drugs, and more parties held her in Fairbanks. I wish she could have come with us, as my new attitude might have helped her. Or it could have been that her mind-set could have pulled me back down. I will never know for sure. But one thing I did know was that I wanted to enter the family business as a bounty hunter more than I had ever wanted just about anything. I knew that studying for and passing the tests would be difficult, but I wasn't going to let anything—including drugs, alcohol, men, or parties—stand in my way. For once I was 100 percent determined to succeed.

Seventeen

★

New Life, New Identity

All my life, I have been identified as either "white trash," "dirt poor," or "drug addict"—or all three. Those are terrible words to identify with, and they do nothing to build a young woman's self-esteem. They are also difficult words to overcome.

One place that I often have trouble overcoming those words, unfortunately, is in church. When members of a congregation first discover that I was an unwed teen mother they are taken aback. Many do not seem to be able to get past this fact of my life and I do not understand that. Should I be thought of as scum for the rest of my life because I became pregnant at age fourteen?

To these people I say, don't look at what I have done, but what I am doing now. Look at what you see of my children. I am the best parent I can be and anyone who meets my daughters can see that they are thriving. They are my proof, so look at my recent successes, rather than use negative words from my past to describe me now.

By the time I returned to Hawai'i this second time I knew that one way or another I was done with those negative words and with those identities. I didn't quite know how I'd shake them, but with every passing day and with every new episode of craziness, I desperately wanted the cycle of addiction, poverty, neglect, and abuse that was riddled throughout my family and my life to stop with me. I have made great strides, but I know that I can never stop working toward that goal. Look at my dad. Against all odds he made a better life for himself and became famous for being a bounty hunter rather than an attempted murderer. If he could change his life, I knew I could change mine.

When I arrived, I once again moved in with Dad and Beth. I was totally strung out, but this time I dedicated my first week to getting the drugs out of my system. It was one of the hardest things I ever had to do. I remember asking my dad when the wanting, the feeling I had to have drugs, would go away. He told me it would never go away, and that was one of the saddest things I ever heard him say.

At the time, Dad and Beth lived in a three-bedroom ranch-style house. When I moved in it required some juggling, and when things settled down Abbie, Travis, and I were in one bedroom, with Cecily and Bonnie Jo in the second. Dad, Beth, and Garry

Boy were in the master. I got the feeling that Beth resented our presence and the need for new bedroom assignments, and she also may have thought I was more trouble than I was worth. I do realize I hadn't done much to impress her or anyone else.

The tight living arrangements also made it difficult for me to get along with Beth. Between moments of loving her, I can't tell you how much I hated Beth when I was growing up. But now with what little maturity I had, I could see another side of her. I wanted to make things right between us, so I went overboard to win her over because I knew her feelings for me were similar to mine for her. But my efforts always seemed to backfire. Even though I tried to be sweet and loving, no matter what I did it still was wrong.

As an example, one day I was sent to the store to get greenhouse tomatoes, and I came back with the vine-ripened kind. For the next twenty minutes I heard how worthless I was. "Do you see the words on the list?" I was asked as the list was held in front of my nose. "Do you see where it says *greenhouse?*" Over and over and over. I felt so embarrassed and useless. I knew I had messed up many times in the past. I don't dispute that at all. And I am sure I was told exactly what kind of tomatoes to get. I messed up there, too. But I wanted Beth, and Dad, to know how hard I was trying. I felt then and feel now that encouragement for the effort I was putting forth, rather than negative reinforcement, would have helped me adjust to my new life. I was trying so hard and getting absolutely no praise. So I just tried harder.

I was also heartbroken that Barbara had to stay in Alaska. In spite of Barbara's drug use and irresponsibility, she was still the older sister I adored and I felt lost without her. Having her around would have made my transition much easier.

While all of this made the upheaval of the move from Alaska to Hawai'i difficult, the most life-changing concept that resulted from moving in with Dad and Beth was having enough food to put on my own plate. In Alaska I had just eaten leftovers from a plate I made for Abbie. I never had enough food, and I wanted to be sure Abbie had eaten her fill first. It seems such a simple thing, but I had been so destitute that eating had become a luxury.

One day not too long after I arrived I went along with Beth and Dad and the kids to the beach. I still loved the ocean but hadn't had much time to spend near it, so this was a real treat for me. On the way we stopped at a grocery store to stock up on food for the day. Dad told all of us to be sure to get what we wanted. I think I picked up one pizza Lunchables for Abbie and me to share for the entire day. In my mind, at the time, it seemed like a lot of food for the two of us. But both Dad and Beth asked if I wasn't hungry. I was, but it was such a huge culture shock for me to go into a grocery store and walk out with enough food to fill me for an entire day. I was so happy to have food for both of us that I wanted to cry.

I knew that making the commitment to my new life was going to be hard, but I had not factored in the emotional turmoil it would bring. When I sank to rock bottom it was a gradual process, and I didn't realize how far down I had gone. I could deal with each comfort that was taken away (such as electricity, a bed to sleep in, clean clothing, and food) because it happened over a period of months. But to have all of that back at once was such an overload it was very hard to process. I am grateful to Dad and Beth for taking Abbie and me in and giving me another chance because I shudder to think what might have happened to us if they had not opened their door to us.

But aren't parents supposed to do that? The years of abuse, neglect, and dysfunction from my parents were what had turned me into an addict in the first place. I sometimes felt bad taking up their breathing room, but there's a totem pole to the Chapman family, and I was on the bottom. Because of our family structure, I'd always felt I was groveling, even though I was helping as much as I could. Of course, no one ever let me forget the horrible lie I had told about my dad. I felt like I was continually walking on eggshells.

The last time I was going to use, Dad and Beth were out of town. I really wanted some crack, even though I also wanted to stay clean. The pull toward drugs won out, and by the time I scored the drug I was shaking so badly that it felt as if I had already smoked it. But I hadn't. Instead, I went to Dad's office, where some of the people there were in AA, and I hoped they would help me.

When I walked in I said, "I bought crack today, and all I want to do is go home and smoke it. Please help me." Tayshea had become a good friend, and she dropped everything to share her story of recovery with me. Her tough love and kind words allowed me to go home and flush the crack down the toilet. I have never looked back. Thank you, Tayshea.

Once the worst of the drugs had left my system my head felt clearer and I had more energy. Those, however, did not come easily. Going without drugs was terribly hard and felt alien to me. At first just getting through each day was an enormous challenge. My body craved the drugs it had been used to for so long. I really wanted to use, but I wanted to be clean for Abbie and for myself even more.

Eventually I began helping Beth around the house. In fact, I became an overachiever. After years of "underperforming" nearly everything I attempted in life, I began to excel. I once again started to get the kids up for school, made their breakfast, dropped them off, and picked them up. I also did routine household chores such as vacuuming, cooking, and laundry. I made sure the bathrooms were spotless, the kids' clothes were folded to perfection, and I correctly picked up every item from the grocery store.

My biggest problem, once I was past the withdrawals, was learning to have fun again. For so many years my fun was to do drugs. Now I had to find different ways to unwind. I began to run, and before I knew it I was up to six miles a day. I also spent a lot of "fun time" with Abbie. I took her to the zoo, and to the beach park near us. Our part of Alaska had been small, and there weren't a lot of things to do the three months of the year when it was actually warm enough to go outside, so I reveled in the many outdoor activities Hawai'i had to offer. I also got caught up on all the movies I had missed.

In addition, I began working in our bail bonds office, Da Kine, and I liked the work right away. It was interesting, and I felt I was helping people. It had been so long since I'd been able to think about anything other than mere survival that helping a stranger out of a jam gave me another kind of high altogether.

The first thing I realized about my new job was that I had a new identity as Dog's daughter. Gone were the old, derogatory labels I used to identify with. As Dad's daughter I was able to claim a tiny bit of respect for myself, and that helped boost my self-esteem.

All of this helped me realize that I did not have to be a drug addict for the rest of my life. That was a really empowering thought. I had been using drugs for ten years, more than half my life. Now I finally realized that I had the power within myself to be a person who didn't use. Even more important, I could live a much better life without drugs than with. I grew up with drugs being all I knew, and every adult around me used. When that is all you know, that is what you become. This was the first opportunity I'd had to prove to myself that there was another way to live, and I grabbed on to that thought with everything I had.

I also realized that because I had been a criminal through my drug use, I could relate to the druggies and other criminals who were our clients in the bail bonds office. Unless I chose to tell them of my past, the people we posted bonds for often did not relate well to me. For once I felt I had something I could control, and that was knowledge. My new level of self-esteem allowed me the option to tell a client about my past—or not. When I did, most times I could change the way they looked at me and felt about me. Knowing that I had been able to get off the street gave hope to many people who walked in our door. Knowing I could make a difference with just a few words was powerful, and I knew that somehow I wanted to dedicate my life to helping others. I just didn't know how I would do that—yet.

When it came to the *Dog the Bounty Hunter* show, however, at first I was really shy. *International* television? It scared the crap out of me to realize that millions and millions of people would see me. I also did not feel at all comfortable around the cameras that, during filming, were around all day every day. I'm sure you can imagine how hard it is to act normal when a huge lens is held a foot away from your face.

Part of my discomfort with the show was because I didn't feel I had a place on the team and didn't feel I had anything to contribute. But as I gained experience I got traction as a map expert and navigator. When that happened, when I knew I was really helping, I felt like I went from assisting Beth to having a real job. I began going to the office every day and also began stocking up on gadgets of my own because I had already learned that every bounty hunter needs his or her own supply of handcuffs, flashlights, and the like.

Having the right gear was important to my success in my new job. Whatever I had done in life I had always wanted to do well.

Bail bonds and bounty hunting were no different. I wanted to be good at this. Really good. I thought back to the day I received the visit from Child Protective Services, when they checked up on baby Abbie. Even though I had to wash clothes in a tub and dry them with a fan in front of the fireplace, my baby was clean and healthy. I did the best I could with what I had and I was proud of that, just as I was beginning to be proud of my new career.

One of the biggest mistakes I made in my life was not continuing my formal education. I loved learning, and considering my circumstances when I was in school, I earned good grades. But school was just too hard after Abbie was born. Having dropped out, I had a hard time getting any kind of a job. People see my ninth-grade education and immediately assume I am dumb. My commitment to doing a job well and my love of learning meant that when I realized I could become licensed in bail bonds I jumped at the chance. I studied hard and ended up having to take the written test several times before I passed. It was a frustrating time, but I didn't give up. This was an opportunity that was important to me. My efforts paid off, and soon I was the youngest licensed bail bonds agent in Hawai'i. That I had accomplished one of my goals was hugely empowering to me and helped me stay focused on the new path I had mapped out for my life.

I was eighteen years old when I became licensed. If there had been a licensing process for bounty hunting I would have gone after that, too. The state of Hawai'i, however, does not require any licensing of bounty hunters, as some other states do.

I still like bail bonds better than bounty hunting, but in our family it is hard to do one without the other. A lot of my most memorable bounty hunts have aired on various episodes of *Dog the Bounty Hunter*, but there is one bounty hunt that I wish had aired on the show because it kept us on our toes. The only reason it didn't air was because we didn't get our man, but it wasn't for lack of trying. And that's the thing about what we do. We are not always successful. On *Dog the Bounty Hunter*, footage shows us going out and eventually making a successful capture, but there are hundreds of hours of footage that have never been used because we either never found our subject, or he or she got away. That's how it worked on our reality show.

In this particular bounty, Kris, a young Asian man, had $200,000 worth of warrants. No matter how you look at it, that's a lot of money. We chased this guy all over town for weeks, camera crew in tow. Finally we tracked down his girlfriend's ex-boyfriend who said Kris occasionally crashed on his couch.

After several days of on-and-off conversation, our ex-boyfriend informant gave us a tip that Kris would be at a nearby McDonald's that evening. At this point we just had a skeleton crew available. There was a producer and two camera guys. Dad and Beth were out of town, so Big Travis (father of Barbara's son), my brother Leland, and I got in place well before our guy was supposed to show up.

At the appointed time we saw our informant pull into the parking lot, talk briefly with our escapee, and then leave. The subject was in an old Jeep Cherokee, and we had been told the vehicle had bad brakes. Obviously, the more information we can get like this, the better. We may not need it but you never know what odd tidbit may become useful, or even save one of us from getting hurt.

We had two vehicles, one idling in front of the other. Leland was in front and I was in the second car. When the subject began to pull away, Leland and I both began talking on our radios together. The result was that neither of us could tell what the other was saying—or intending to do. By this time we were in the middle of an intersection, and our subject was getting away.

Just as I radioed Leland to see what he wanted me to do I saw him ram his car into the fleeing subject's vehicle. I tried to hem the guy in from the other side. Oddly enough, Leland had just returned from taking a class at Blackwater (the US Training Center) on "pit maneuvers," so he was putting his new driving training into action. Before I could stop, Leland jumped out of his car and ran to Kris's car, Mace in hand.

In the confusion, our cameraman fell out of my car and onto the street. My bumper and license plate were dragging, and by the time Leland got back into his car, having missed his Mace opportunity, the subject was pulling away. I wanted to go back and pick up our cameraman, but Leland was already in hot pursuit and told me to leave him. We probably looked to outsiders like some kind of cartoon characters. All our efforts were to no avail, however, as our guy managed to get away.

The worst part of it was that Leland and I then had to call Dad to tell him about the wrecked cars and that our guy got away. I can tell you there were a lot of other phone calls I would rather have made! If that wasn't bad enough, several weeks later the subject got into a showdown with the Hawai'i State Police, and they were the ones to apprehend him instead of us. If we don't get our guy, we don't get paid.

I'm glad Kris was returned to custody, although, of course, I was really bummed that after all our hard work someone else made the capture. After all, part of my ability to recover a sense of self-esteem that I either lost early in life or never developed at all is to feel that I make a meaningful contribution to our family business. I know this work may seem bizarre to the TV viewing public at times, but at the heart of all the hype and strange behavior, bounty hunting is still all about making the public safer by getting wanted criminals off the streets.

My dad attributes his hunting skills to his father and his love for hunting wildlife, but I believe he has something much more special than that. I remember being on the hunt for one man in an episode of *Dog the Bounty Hunter* and his sister convinced us that our suspect was not in the house. However, Dad kept saying, "I feel him. I know he is in there."

Just as Dad suspected, the man was home, hiding in a closet. How did Dad know? He has a gift and his bounty hunting skills are the greatest of any man in the world. I like to think that I inherited at least some of those skills. My years on *Dog the Bounty Hunter* were some of the greatest times of my life. Spending time with my family, long car rides, and the bonding we did was happiness beyond measure. I loved being part of the posse, and loved that we brought a new adventure every week to millions of fans. But most of all, I'm so grateful that I had the chance to be a part of my father's dream.

Eighteen

★

Love and Loss

The autumn of 2005 and winter of 2006 I spent learning the ins and outs of the bail bonds and bounty hunting business. I realized that I had absorbed a lot when I was living with my dad as a child, so I used this knowledge as my base and expanded from there.

A lot of the business is instinct. What do you feel about the person who wants to make bail? What does your gut say about where a bounty might be hiding? This even extends to how you treat the person. Some need hard-core language and physicality before they realize the seriousness of their situation, while others need a pat on the back and some encouraging words. You'd better know which to give right away because if you are wrong, you could be in a lot of trouble.

I also spent that time getting reacquainted with my family. Six years is a long time to be away from people you love, especially when you are a teenager for most of that time. Everyone had changed and matured, including me. I especially loved getting to know my little brother and sister, Garry Boy and Bonnie Jo. Things had smoothed out between us since our first introduction, and I felt blessed to be part of their lives. Among other opportunities, I found that the kids often took time to talk to me about what was going on with them during our rides in the car to and from their various schools. It was, and is, a wonderful way to bond.

★

Sometime early in 2006 I pulled up at a traffic light, looked at the car next to me, and saw Bo Galanti. Bo was part of my AA group of friends. He had begun doing odd jobs for my dad, and I had seen him many times at Dad's and around town since my return to Hawai'i.

On this particular day Dad and Beth were out of town and I was taking care of all the kids. I had come down with a bad cold a few days before, and when Bo learned I was sick he invited himself over to help. That evening he helped with dinner and the next day helped with some household shopping. Bo was impressed that I did all the cooking, cleaning, and child care in my dad's home, especially because he was a single dad to a young daughter himself.

That fact was attractive to me, and a month or so later, after he shyly asked me for a kiss, we began dating.

Our dating wasn't as simple as two people wanting to be together, though. I first had to get permission from Dad and Beth. When I had come back to Hawai'i, Beth had set up a lot of restrictions on my life, and dating was one of these. I know she felt that rigid structure of my days would help me in my recovery, and I am sure it did. But now that I had been back for more than a year and was doing very well I was finding many of the restrictions too rigid. After all, I had turned nineteen the previous June, and according to the law I was a legal adult.

I was a little nervous about asking Dad and Beth about dating Bo, though, because while I wasn't sure how old he was, I knew he was older than I. I was sure Dad and Beth would look at the age difference, think of Brendan, and say no. But I was to be surprised. Instead Dad said, "Sure. We know Bo, and he's a great guy." I was so excited!

Bo and I quickly became inseparable and I learned that Bo's daughter, Serene, had been born the previous fall. You don't see single dads caring for infant daughters very often, and I was amazed at how sweet Bo was with Serene. His love and affection for her were obvious, and I thought he was so handsome.

One day I went to Bo's house and found him crying. Serene wasn't eating and Bo was terrified that she was ill, so I asked him to show me. When Bo tried to shove a spoonful of peas into Serene's firmly closed mouth, I said, "Serene is only six months old. She doesn't need to eat all that much." And with those words, right then and there I decided to take this man and baby and make them into a family with Abbie and me.

I had gone an entire year without doing drugs or dating, which—considering my background and the women in my life who always had to have a physical relationship with a man—was something of a record. During that year I had begun to develop dreams and goals of my own. One big goal was to have a home for lost teen girls, girls who were pregnant and had nowhere to go, girls who were beaten down by life and who had no hope of making good choices because none had been made for them. Any man I took into my life would have to support that dream, and Bo did.

I was also impressed that Bo was not intimidated that I was Dog's daughter. My dad by this time was an international star, and many men were afraid to approach me because of that. Of course, Dad's reputation as a tough guy figured into that mix, too, but Bo had come from a tough background himself. I am sorry to say that he was a victim of childhood beatings by his father. I also didn't see Bo attaching himself to me because I was a regular cast member of *Dog the Bounty Hunter,* as many other men might have. The fame that goes along with a successful television program was the main enticement to some men who were interested in dating me. I was so pleased that I had matured enough to understand that, and that I could now deflect that kind of interest without too much trouble.

Before my sobriety, I would have "needed" attention from men, no matter what the reason. But now I knew that if someone wanted to be close to me only because I was on television, then I had zero interest in being with him. Being on TV was what I did. It wasn't who I was.

★

While my love with Bo was new, Dad and Beth were ready to take their love to a new level. A wedding was in the works, and it was going to be captured for the show. We were all so excited. Dad and Beth had been together for more than a decade as a couple and had known each other far longer than that.

The wedding was scheduled for Saturday, May 20, 2006. The Hilton Waikoloa Resort and Spa in Kona on the Big Island was booked for the big day, and invitations for the more than two hundred guests were sent. If you think details of a regular wedding are hard to pull together, imagine the added details of coordinating them for a reality television show. Beth and the A&E producers were huddled together for months making sure the day would go exactly according to plan.

Among the first portions of the wedding festivities were the rehearsal and the rehearsal dinner. Both were amazing. Beth had purchased new outfits for all of Dad's kids, including those of us who were adults. For the dinner we had an outdoor clambake and a live band, and we all danced the night away. I remember being so happy. I was on top of the world that night with a wonderful career, the show was going strong, and I was in love with the man of my dreams. It remains one of the best times of my life.

But after the rehearsal dinner nothing, nothing at all, went as planned.

The morning of Dad's wedding I was in my hotel room when the phone rang. I checked the caller ID and saw it was my mother. I didn't want to deal with her this early on my dad's wedding day, so I didn't answer. But a minute later the phone rang again. I knew if she called back it must be important, so I answered and was surprised to find John on the other end of the line. "Lyssa," he said, "the troopers just left. Your sister was in a terrible car accident and she didn't make it."

Just like that, my safe, secure, happy little world dropped out from under my feet. Barbara was gone? It couldn't be. But I knew by the somber tone of John's voice that it was. The big sister who had taken such good care of me when she was just a child, the wise sister I once turned to for advice, love, comfort, and guidance, was dead. She was just twenty-three.

I went outside, fell onto the ground, and screamed, "No, no, *no!*" as tears streamed down my face. I later learned that Barbara was riding in a stolen SUV the evening before with a guy named Scott Standefer when the vehicle left the roadway, hit an embankment, rolled, crashed into some trees, and landed upside down. Both Barbara and Scott were killed.

I thought of the night before, when we had all been dancing so happily. Little did we know that Barbara was already dead. How could I have not recognized that? She was my sister. I should have felt something when she left this earth.

I was shaking, and hysterical with grief, but I knew I had to tell my dad and Beth. But first I went inside to tell Bo. It took a few minutes for me to dress and gather myself together; then I walked down the hallway of our hotel to deliver the devastating news. All the way I kept thinking, "this can't be happening," "this isn't real," "what kind of nightmare is this?"

In the previous months, I had asked Dad many times to bring Barbara down for the wedding, but he wouldn't hear any talk of it. At first he said there was no room, or that she had legal issues in Alaska that kept her from attending. But I think that he and Beth didn't want her drug use or her sometimes wild behavior to ruin the big day. It was his way of practicing tough love, but that morning I thought that if she had been here with us, with her family, she might still be living on earth. Now I realize that only God knows the answer to that.

Just before I got to the honeymoon suite where Dad and Beth were staying I ran into a friend of Beth's. She could tell I was upset, and when I relayed the news she said, "You can't tell Beth; it's her wedding day."

Those words infuriated me. It may have been Beth's wedding day, but my dad deserved to know that his daughter was dead. Before I could knock on the door of the suite, however, Beth came around the corner of the hall. When I told her the news she cried, "Oh, f— no. No! Not today." Then Beth opened the door to the two-story suite and went upstairs to tell Dad.

The deafening silence lasted for a full minute, then another. Then I heard a gut-wrenching scream from my dad, followed by "Not my Barbara Katie. My Barbara Katie!" Barbara was Dad's oldest daughter, and I know he loved her from the bottom of his heart.

I can't begin to explain to you how distressed I was by Barbara's passing. The sadness I felt was beyond anything I had ever known. It was heartbreaking to me that I had found my way out of the dysfunction of my upbringing but Barbara hadn't. Why hadn't I done more to help her? Why hadn't anyone done more? Survivor's guilt kicked in like a sucker punch to my stomach. Why was I the one who was on the show and not Barbara? Why was I the one who had gotten her life together? But I didn't have time to deal with any of that. I had a wedding to attend.

After the initial shock, Dad called everyone to the patio: Beth, Leland, Duane Lee, Cecily, the entire A&E production team and crew, a few others, and me. I saw another side of my brothers that day as they all cried huge tears of true grief. I hadn't known that they had loved Barbara so much.

There was a lot of emotional discussion of rescheduling the wedding, and most of the people lamented, "Why did it have to happen now, of all times?" My thought was that we should at least take the day to mourn Barbara and recover from the shock—move the wedding to the next day. All of the guests and crew would still be there. But when cameras are involved, moving a wedding is not that easy. A&E had spent a lot of money on the wedding, and Dad really wanted to marry Beth. "God doesn't kill your daughter to stop you from getting married," Dad eventually said to Duane Lee. That quote ended up as part of the *Dog the Bounty Hunter* episode that covered the wedding. I couldn't forget even then that cameras recorded *every* part of our lives.

The wedding was held as planned.

Dad and the Reverend Tim Storey arrived by water on a platform between two canoes. Dad was dressed all in white and looked very striking. Beth carried a huge bouquet of peach and white flowers and was teary-eyed as she walked down the aisle at the foot of the hotel's grand staircase. Dad, overcome with emotion, walked partway up the aisle to greet her.

After, at the reception, Dad told the guests about Barbara and that our family wanted the reception to be a celebration of both Dad and Beth's marriage, and Barbara's life. As you can imagine, it was an emotional event and there were lots of hugs and tears amid the smiles.

I took the opportunity to get drunk. Barbara had always said that when she died she wanted everyone to have a big party, so I guessed this was it. After, I immediately went home to Oahu. Since then, we sometimes go to the Big Island on business. Dad and Beth usually stay in the same room they did for their wedding. As for me, I can't even stay in the same hotel. I guess everyone grieves differently.

The wedding took place on May 20, and the last time I had spoken to Barbara was on May 17. By this time Barbara was shooting drugs into her system with needles, and she was upset that she and Tucker were the only of Dad's children who had not been invited. (Tucker wasn't invited because he was in prison.) Barbara told me she had gotten in the habit of sleeping on her stomach on top of all her possessions because the people she was around stole things from her when she slept. I wanted to put little Travis on the phone, but she said no. It was too hard to hear his voice. Too depressing. That was the last time I talked to her.

Knowing that little Travis was not in the car with my sister got me through that terrible time. But I was conflicted because I also knew that without Travis, Barbara had gone completely off track. I remember praying, and God telling me that He was so sorry that Barbara had to go. He told me He was also sorry that I was so sad now but that Barbara was no longer in pain and was happy.

I've also dreamed about Barbara. She told me not to feel bad for her; she was with our grandmother and all of our former dogs. In fact, she said she felt bad for me because I was still here on earth.

Since then I often have a recurring nightmare of walking through the Valley of Death and fighting off all kinds of horrible things before emerging to a beautiful place. In my waking hours I feel strongly connected to Barbara's presence every day. Barbara had always loved butterflies, and now whenever I see a butterfly I feel like she is still around.

★

Bo was my rock as he comforted me in my bottomless grief. He was at the hotel with me when we learned the news and he said all the right things to keep me functioning as best I could, even later, when the media wouldn't leave us alone. Whenever I was ready to try to move on I'd see yet another headline: DOG'S DAUGHTER KILLED IN STOLEN CAR. I was as broken as I had ever been, but it was during this time that the love and kindness Bo directed toward me filled me with the desire to be married to him. I was thrilled that he felt the same way; it just took time and a near disaster to get there.

On Valentine's Day 2007, Bo asked me to be his wife. I had found the ring in his sock drawer some weeks earlier and knew he was going to ask. I just didn't know when or where. We had spent part of the day at Dad and Beth's, and I got the feeling he was going to ask when we were there, but it didn't feel right to me, so I kept myself busy. After we got home, however, Bo began rubbing my feet while we were sitting on the couch. He then professed his love for Abbie and me and asked me to be his wife. I was thrilled to accept!

Four days later, however, tragedy almost struck. Dad and Beth had gone out of town, and we were watching the kids. Before they left, Beth cautioned me to watch Bo's daughter, Serene, around the pool. Dad and Beth had just given Serene, who was eighteen months old, a princess makeup kit complete with shoes that clacked all over the house when she wore them. After Dad and Beth left, we checked all the sliding doors in the house that opened to the pool and sat down to watch a movie. I was comforted by the clack-clack sound of Serene walking through the house—until I realized I didn't hear the sound anymore. Bo and I jumped up and ran through the house. The last room we checked was Dad and Beth's bedroom, and there we found the slider open to the pool.

Our worst nightmare was realized when we saw Serene floating facedown on top of the water. Bo jumped to her and flailed the arms of her limp, seemingly lifeless body wildly after he got her onto the patio. I screamed for Cecily to call 911 and dropped to my knees to pray.

Then the most amazing thing happened. Two pictures popped into my head, one of Barbara and one of a tiny casket, and then a voice in my head said, "Get up off your butt and go over there and help that baby." I had taken a CPR class in seventh grade and somehow remembered what to do, so I took Serene from Bo, tilted her head back, pinched her nose, and breathed into her.

I couldn't feel the air go into her, though; it was as if Serene was already dead. But I kept breathing, then I did a bunch of chest pumps, and then I breathed some more. Finally Serene threw up a bunch of water. I picked her up and ran for the gate at the end of Dad's driveway, hoping to get her to the emergency personnel who were on their way a fraction of a second sooner.

The firefighters who showed up just about then told me I had saved Serene's life. We feel that she had been without oxygen for two to three minutes, and the only lingering damage was a sensitivity to chlorine, which has decreased as she has gotten older. I can honestly say that while I am glad I know how to do it, performing CPR is one thing I hope I *never* have to do again.

We had a second little "God" moment that day. Travis, Garry Boy, and Abbie had been playing in Garry's room, and inexplicably the doorknob jammed right about the time Serene fell into the pool, locking them all in. It is such a blessing to me that these kids did not have to witness Serene's apparently lifeless body or the frantic activities of Bo and me as we desperately tried to keep her from leaving us.

Even though I did not give birth to Serene, something of me jumped inside her that day and bonded us. And I am so thankful to Barbara for giving me the jump start to go to Serene and help her. If not for my sister's words from heaven, Serene might not be with us today.

One weekend in the first part of 2007, I agreed to up my commitment to Bo and move in with him. While I would do things very differently today, in my mind back then the next step in our engagement was living together. Actually, I had waited this long only because it had been made clear to Bo and me that if we moved in together, little Travis would stay with Dad and Beth.

I also knew that Dad and Beth wouldn't approve of our cohabitation if we were not married, even though they themselves had lived together for many years before they were married. So in the middle of the night I packed up Abbie's and my things and moved in with Bo and Serene. I was thrilled to become a surrogate mother to Serene, as I didn't want her to grow up without a mom, as I had in my early years. Bo was very good to Abbie, too, and I was so deeply in love that I thought I had found the perfect man. Unfortunately, perfect men, perfect people, do not exist.

Nineteen

★

A Baby and a Good-Bye

I *loved being married to* Bo, and I adored being a mom to Serene. Even though we don't use the word in our family, inside I have felt either like a "step" child or "step" sibling all my life. The word "step" also made me feel like I was half of something. I was half a daughter, half a sister, half an aunt. I was never a whole or all of any kind of relationship.

I knew there were a lot of barriers in raising children who were not biologically yours. With Travis, who was as much my child as anyone's, I loved him and then he was taken away, then I was able to love him once more, then he was gone again. Over and over this cycle repeated itself. Sometimes Travis left with Barbara, other times he was with Dad and Beth, and sometimes he was with his own dad. It was traumatic for him and heart-wrenching for me.

I didn't want Serene to have to go through that, so I put all thoughts of the words "step" and "half" out of my head and raised and loved her as my own. To this day she calls me Mom. The first thing I did was put Serene in the private all-girls Catholic school that Abbie went to. Abbie was just five, but had attended a preschool there since she was three. We were not Catholic, but the school was by far the best school I could find. In addition to reading, writing, and arithmetic, they taught good values and encouraged the development of social skills, athletics, music, and art. Cecily and Bonnie Jo also attended the school.

As you may recall, I was already expecting when Bo and I married. As my due date grew near I compared this pregnancy experience to the one I had with Abbie. Really, there was no comparison. For this baby I had a nice home that included a dad. I had a drug-free life and plenty of food. For me it was the great American Dream. All I had ever wanted was a home with a mom and a dad, and lots of kids to sit around the dinner table with. All of that was coming true, but it had taken an emotional roller coaster to get here.

Late in 2008 I had gone off my birth control pills for two short weeks to regulate my system and start a new kind of pill. When I began the new pills from the first week on, I didn't feel right. I went to my doctor and she suggested we wait another month. When I didn't have my period in November of that year I began to get worried. The day before Christmas I bought a home pregnancy test, used it, and went into our bedroom to read it by myself.

When the test turned out to be positive I cried my eyes out. I was so devastated that I dropped to my knees. Bo and I weren't married at this point and I had struggled as a single mom to Abbie. Even though my life was much better now, I knew how hard it was for both the baby and the mom when they were on their own. I didn't want to put another baby through all of that hardship.

Eventually I wiped the tears off my face, put on a happy face for Bo, and went out to the living room. "Let's go read the test," I said with a fake smile. Fortunately, Bo was thrilled that he was going to be a dad again.

I was still taking care of my younger brothers and sister at Dad's house, but by this time I was also serving as an assistant of sorts to Beth. My duties often kept me there until eight or nine at night. Plus when we were filming the show, the hours could run much later than that. I knew that as my pregnancy progressed it would be too much, so as Bo washed the dishes one night I called Beth. "Guess what?" I said brightly. "I have good news. I'm pregnant." I was hoping for some celebratory words of joy, but what I got instead was, "That will be *great* for the ratings!"

I mentioned to Bo that maybe we ought to get married before I got too big with the baby. Even though I wanted a beach wedding, we initially tried to pull together a quickie wedding in Las Vegas, but everything from the flowers to the venue fell apart. Then Beth suggested that we get married on the show. It made sense. We lived in paradise. Why not have a beautiful wedding at home? So that's what we did.

I was fourteen weeks pregnant on the day of my wedding on February 20, 2009, and while I was completely head over heels in love, it wasn't too long before I began to see some red flags. At this point, however, the flags were nothing more than a vague warning, but it wouldn't take long for them to turn into a full-blown hurricane.

★

My pregnancy progressed with a few hitches. Bo went with me to the first doctor's appointment and never went to another. He also never touched my stomach after that appointment, not ever, until after the baby was born. I know he wanted our child, but his lack of touch made me feel unsupported and unloved. I also began spotting after a hike on the Big Island and was confined to bed rest for several weeks. My inability to be mobile didn't help our film schedule, but by the time I was seven months along I was back in full force, albeit reluctantly.

Bounty hunting is a physical and dangerous job, and I didn't feel comfortable doing it in the later stages of pregnancy. On one hunt we were going after a heroin addict. In the process I ended up in the backseat of a car with an informant during a high-speed chase. I was terrified for my baby, and after, I called Bo. I was nearly hysterical and insisted that I wanted to quit the show. Bo calmed me down, and I resumed filming other episodes.

Our beautiful daughter, Madalynn Grace Galanti, was born

on August 7, 2009. Bo and I were both instantly besotted with this amazing golden-haired child. As I mentioned before, the production crew filmed the entire birth for the show. In an ideal world, I would have preferred them not to be there for that important private moment with our little family, but everyone involved convinced me that our viewers would like to share that experience, so I acquiesced.

While I was pregnant, Bo and Beth had numerous conversations about how the birth could be filmed tastefully, then made the decision to do it. This was after Dad and Beth were offered a "bonus" for the exclusive rights, and Bo learned that we would get part of it. The birth of our child was the first time I realized that money was so important to Bo.

Later, as I watched the show as it aired, I felt exploited. I know the viewers enjoyed the episode, as we got tons of positive e-mail and Twitter and Facebook posts about it, and I was happy about that part of it. But I'm still not sure why I didn't insist that the birth not be filmed. It would have been my right to do so. I could have asked my doctor to clear the room, and today I would have done so without a second thought. All I can say is that I wasn't there yet. I had made great strides in my recovery and in developing some self-esteem, but I was not where I needed to be. Not yet, anyway.

★

After the birth I was prescribed and took codeine for the pain. I had not been high since I was eighteen years old, but the codeine took me there right away. After the birth I also had issues with my body image, as I had gained more than 100 pounds during my pregnancy. I don't know exactly how much I gained because when I reached 190 pounds, I stopped weighing myself. I do know that I gained a lot of weight after that. When I took the codeine, however, all the bad feelings about my body went away. In fact, I felt wonderful! Sadly, I didn't have any idea that I was in a dangerous situation with my addiction. After all, I reasoned, the doctor had prescribed these pills to me. I was *supposed* to be taking them.

Relatively quickly, I dropped to 150 pounds, which was still about 50 pounds too much for me. Then I plateaued. No matter what I did, I could not drop another pound. I didn't have too much time to think about that, though, because I had a baby to take care of.

After we got Mady home I was pleased to realize that I was a far better mom to Mady as an infant than I had been to Abbie. I had come a long way! But when Mady was just a month old, she began running a high temperature. Concerned, I took her to Queens Hospital in Honolulu on September 11, 2009. This was against the advice of my family and husband. They all thought I was overreacting. The people on staff at the hospital agreed with me, however. In fact, they suspected meningitis and wanted to do a spinal tap.

When I heard that news I began to feel that my life was starting to spin me out of control. It was a feeling I often had when Abbie was small, and I was overwhelmed. A spinal tap? On my one-month-old baby? Some of my feelings may have been from the codeine I was taking and some of it might have been true fear. Some of my roller coaster emotions might have been hormones from the birth—and from breast-feeding. Or they might have caused by stress from having a husband who had two jobs and no money, or being on camera almost one hundred pounds heavier than I had been a few months before.

Needing support, I called Beth, and when she came we asked if we could see another doctor. The original doctor was at the tail end of her shift and was worn out. I did not feel comfortable having her do the spinal tap when she was obviously exhausted. We asked to wait until the next doctor arrived but were told we couldn't do that. This doctor, apparently, had to do the spinal. Instead, I decided to take Mady home and find a different doctor the next day.

Leaving wasn't as simple as walking out the door, though. When Beth and I tried to leave the hospital a few minutes later, security would not agree to bring our cars around unless we left Mady with them. They were that serious about her health, and their attitude just scared me all the more. We were able to leave only after Beth took out her iPhone and began filming members of the security staff who were harassing us. Then I took Mady to her pediatrician, who suggested I give the fever one more day before making any decisions about what to do.

That evening I lay in bed with Mady and prayed with everything I had that she would be okay. The next morning, when

Mady was no better, I left Bo asleep in bed and took Mady back to our pediatrician, who encouraged me to take Mady to Kapiolani Women's and Children's Hospital. They ended up doing a spinal tap. Mady's veins were so small that it took them seven tries to get the needle in. They'd pat her feet, her ankles, her hands, and her arms very hard to try to get her veins to come up. She was screaming and screaming and I was so upset a staff member gave me some Ativan to decrease my growing anxiety.

Mady was hospitalized for a week—a week during which Bo was very absent—and during which I took both codeine and Ativan the entire time. Tests on Mady's cloudy spinal fluid had come back positive for meningitis, an infection of the membranes that cover the brain and spinal cord. They didn't yet know if it was bacterial or viral in nature, but started Mady on antibiotics out of caution. While I was getting high and spending every second of the day with Mady in the hospital, Serene and Abbie were with Big Travis (Travis's father), and Bo got himself a tattoo of a scorpion.

I was devastated by my family's lack of support. Mady was hospitalized from September 12 through September 20. During that time Bo and Cecily each brought me food and visited once. No one else came.

Beth had scheduled a photo shoot for season six in California on September 28. Because I was breast-feeding I had no choice but to fly with Mady to the shoot. In addition, I was still huge, and wardrobe had my old measurements. Nothing they brought in even came close to fitting. It was beyond embarrassing. I was still about 150 pounds, but I am normally a tiny person and am just five feet tall. Beth at that time was thinner than I was, so I wore Beth's clothes for the shoot.

While I can't be positive, I think Mady began having breathing difficulties at the shoot. Dad is a chain-smoker and smoked throughout the session. I think the smoke from the cigarettes was the start of Mady's second round of hospitalization.

Two days after we got home Mady came down with pneumonia. Back in the hospital she had a second spinal tap, but this time we had good news: the fluid was clear. There was a second round of IVs and antibiotics, but during the ten days we were there this time, absolutely no one came to see us.

To me, this was just another sign that my irrevocable act, my allowing the adults around me to assume it was Dad who molested me, will never be forgotten. Everyone throughout my life had always said what a screwed-up mess I was, but by now I had realized that was not true. I was a good mom, a good person. I had come a long way. Maybe, I thought, if my family could not support me at a time like this, they were the ones who were screwed up.

I slept both hospital stays on a pullout chair and was up each time the doctors came in for their every-two-hour check on Mady. By the seventh or eighth day I was so exhausted I snapped at a new doctor who came in early one morning after a shift change and chased her out of the room. I had been up with Mady all night and hadn't slept in several days.

A month later we were all in Colorado for Thanksgiving to

film a Christmas special. Between the birth, Mady's illnesses, my horrendous weight gain, keeping up a public image, taping episodes of the show, and my family's total lack of support, it was a lot to handle. And I managed it all in completely the wrong way, by taking more pills.

★

On New Year's Eve that Year Bo and I went out with Duane Lee and his girlfriend. I was still really upset about my body image and my inability to lose weight and had decided to get a breast enhancement after the holidays. Bo had been "hands off" for months now, and I thought the surgery would make me more attractive to him.

I was in the shower in the Waikiki hotel room Bo and I had taken for the night when we somehow got into a huge fight. One reason I don't remember the start of the fight is that we had been drinking, and I hadn't drunk anything for years. Bo ended up throwing his wedding ring at me and smacking me in the head. Terrified, I locked the bathroom door, but Bo is a big guy and he broke the door down and pulled me out of the shower by my neck, then held me captive against the wall.

When I was able to break free I called security. I wanted Bo out of the room. Our family had had Cecily's birthday party there the previous June, and when I told security I wanted the police involved they said no. They reasoned that because I was Dog's daughter, bringing the police into it could take the situation completely out of hand. Instead, they helped me out of the room and I went home without Bo.

That was the first time my husband ever laid hands on me, but it was not the last. It all fell into place for me then, way too late. In the months we had been married, Bo had had some very angry outbursts, and I realized that I had become an abused spouse, with all of the ugly things that term implies.

After the New Year's incident I was prescribed more painkillers because my neck was messed up. Then, after my breast surgery, I was prescribed Percocet and Valium. I was taking all of these pills every day along with the other pills I had been prescribed. When I ran out, I'd just get refills. It was that easy. I'd also had some dental work done and was prescribed Tylenol 3, then Tylenol 4. Before I knew it, I was hooked on this very dangerous mix of prescription drugs. It got so bad that if I didn't take the pills I would begin to shake.

I was also taking these pills on bounty hunts and while we were filming for the show. During the summer we usually filmed in Colorado, and it was after a Justin Bieber concert there that our entire family went to that things really fell apart. Instead of watching the show, I ended up partying near the buses with Justin's production crew. I should have sat with my family and enjoyed the show. I realized that even then, but by this time my addiction was so out of control it was all I could think about. Pills and booze had completely taken over my life.

After the show, when Bo and I got home to the rental house across the street from Dad's, I took a shower and went to bed, even though I knew Bo was seething with anger. Before I knew what was happening, Bo grabbed me by my feet, pulled me out of bed, and slapped me hard across the face while I was on the bathroom floor. Then he began choking me so hard that I started to black out. My last thought before I lost consciousness was that I was going to die. What would become of my baby girls? When I came to sometime later, Bo was gone.

When Beth came over and learned what had happened she was unwavering in her words: "Bo must go." But I was such a classically abused spouse that I wanted with everything I had to go with him. So I did.

I later learned that my feelings were not unique. Domestic abuse is about control and power and usually involves the abuser getting and keeping control and power over the abused. To simplify, someone who commits domestic abuse is a control freak. An abuser can't feel good unless he feels he is in total control.

The abuser can use physical violence, yelling, screaming, and emotional or sexual abuse to attempt to control. He (or she) can leave physical and emotional scars. Domestic abuse happens to people of all ages, races, and religions, but nearly 95 percent of domestic abuse victims are women. According to the National Coalition Against Domestic Abuse, every fifteen seconds someone becomes a victim of abuse. I was just one of thousands. I knew the abuse had to stop but I wasn't ready to let go of anything. Yet.

A Baby and a Good-Bye

★

Over the next few months my abuse of pills, alcohol, and now drugs (including cocaine) continued. By this time I had turned twenty-one, and guess what? I could now go into a bar legally and order a drink. And I did. Again, and again, and again. Then I realized that I had been taking pills every day since the day Mady was born. Additionally, since I had first been put on Trazodone when I was twelve, I had been using pills to escape the stresses of my life. Now every evening I'd open a drawer in my nightstand that I called my "medicine drawer" and look at all my pretty pills. Then I'd take the perfect combo for that night with a glass of wine. I wanted to stop this negative and destructive behavior. I needed to stop. I had to stop. But I didn't want it badly enough. Not then.

One day, however, I woke up with a clear realization that everything in my life was awful. My marriage was bad, I was tired all day, and I felt so sick that I looked into rehab facilities. Even then, because doctors had prescribed the medications, it was difficult to convince myself that they were not what I needed. I told Bo in passing that I might be addicted, and he threw away everything except my Ativan. All the Percocet, Valium, Tylenol 3s and 4s, and other pills, just like that, were gone.

I called Dad and Beth and told them everything that was going on. Instead of going to rehab, though, I went to their house and spent two weeks in their guesthouse shaking as I went through the withdrawals of getting the pills and the alcohol out of my system.

The first three days I spent sweating and not eating. Every day after that Beth took me on a sunset walk, and I remember missing the euphoric feeling that the pills gave me more than I can say. But I healed. I was clean. I was free.

In September 2010, after yet another altercation, I finally threw Bo out of the house. With the pills out of my system I could finally deal with the abuse, and I had had enough. Serene stayed with me.

Because we both wanted so much for our marriage to work, Bo and I tried couples therapy, and on our fourth session the counselor asked to speak with me alone. "You need to get away from him and end this," she said. I was stunned. Even though I had asked Bo to leave our home, I wasn't ready to end our marriage. With all my heart, I wanted things to work out.

The counselor reinforced how the cycle of abuse affected my family and me. Bo had been physically abused as a child, so he beat me. That behavior was teaching all three of our girls (Abbie, Serene, and Mady) that it was okay for men to hit women. If our relationship continued, then my adorable, sweet little girls could grow up to seek men who abused them.

I still loved Bo very much, but I did not want to destroy my children—or me. It broke my heart when I filed for divorce. After that Bo still regularly showed up on my couch late at night, and I realized I would not be free of him as long as I was a full-time mom to his daughter, Serene. It was too dangerous for my other girls to have Bo in our home regularly, as he was when he came to see Serene.

How can you weigh one little girl's need for stability and a mom against the need for safety for two other little girls? It was a no-win choice, but I knew it was my responsibility as a mom to keep two of my girls safe. Serene is still my daughter and nothing will ever change that. She just lives with her dad.

As you have seen, 2010 was a tumultuous year for me. I ended it by summoning the effort to lose the extra pounds, which I did through dedicated portion control and walking. I didn't deny myself anything; I just ate smaller portions of everything. At first I walked only a few blocks, then a block became a mile and before I knew it I was regularly running up the hundreds of steps that led to the mouth of Koko Head Crater on the east side of Oahu. My record is eighteen minutes, which, if I say so myself, is pretty darn good.

I also vowed never to allow myself to be abused again and set to work making myself believe that vow.

Twenty

★

Moving Forward

After my divorce, I began reading the Bible more, especially the very powerful book of Luke, and doing online research. The result of all of this was that I began to believe that sin is something you feel inside you. It is not what everyone else thinks of you. Because of that I do what I believe pleases God and have repented for my sins. My reading also opened my eyes and ears to the wonderful gifts I have in my beautiful children. They are my legacy, for they are what I will leave behind.

I love talking to God every day and have found that when I do good, then good happens. It is an amazing concept and I try my best to live a good life. I have a lot of young girls and teens who follow me on the show and online. They look up to me, and I never want to do anything that disappoints them. For them, I try to live a worthy life.

My faith supports me always, but especially when we were learning to live apart from Bo and Serene. Adjusting to divorce is hard. Adjusting to it when you have children is harder. Adjusting to single life when you are on international television in front of millions of people worldwide is the hardest yet. But I did it. I made sure my daughters' questions were answered and their needs were met, and I also took time to take care of me.

First I found a perfect condo in a gated community that made me feel that the girls and I were safe. That everyone else in the complex seemed to be sixty or older was a bonus. I love all of my new neighbors.

Then I found an incredible woman named Verna White, who became our nanny. I say "nanny," but that word is so limiting compared to all she does for us. Verna is so much more. She is a mentor and a great mother to her children. Plus, she is everything that I aspire to be. I am so grateful that she has become family, and I trust her completely with my girls. Our beloved nanny shares my values, and Abbie, Mady, and Serene adore her. I can't begin to explain what a load of stress and worry she takes off my shoulders. Knowing my children are safe, protected, and with someone they love during times I can't be with them means everything to me.

As I moved into 2011, life was finally settling down. On camera and off, I continued to be a valuable member of the *Dog the Bounty Hunter* team, and I felt good about my small part in removing bad guys from the streets. As the show moved into its eighth season I realized how big *Dog the Bounty Hunter* had gotten. In addition to airing in the United States and Canada, we were shown in more than a dozen foreign countries. People in Australia, New Zealand, Germany, Italy, Norway, Sweden, and many other countries not only knew who I was, they also knew a lot about me. It was, and is, quite intimidating. And with the advent of social media, our fans kept up on everything I did on the show—and off.

Our fame—or notoriety, if you prefer—made for some interesting interactions here in Hawai'i. I sometimes got a wary reception from waiters in restaurants when I went to lunch with a friend because they thought I was there to send someone back to jail. It was kind of funny to see their reaction when I sat down and asked for a menu. Other people wanted to stop me on the street and talk, or just give me a supportive thumbs-up as I walked by. Some people, however, were jealous and vindictive.

One day in the middle of March 2011 I broke a tooth at lunch. After going to the dentist, I went to a salon to get my nails done and while there, called Duane Lee. "Hey, we're at Hooters," he said. "Come join us." I had dinner there with members of my family, and we were having a nice time together when an illegal substance was added to my drink without my knowledge. I arrived at the restaurant at about six o'clock but have no memory of anything that happened that evening after eight. Nothing.

One minute I was spending time with my family and, from what people tell me, after midnight I was miles away banging on a stranger's door fully believing my children were being held captive inside. You can imagine my deep-seated fear, for I apparently believed my girls were in danger. In the process, I was arrested for criminal property damage and assaulting a police officer. My mug shot was all over the news the next day, and I have to say, the photo was not my best.

Reconstructing the evening took many conversations with family and friends. As best as I can tell, this is what happened. I left Dad's friend Chris Pollack and Duane Lee at the bar at Hooters, while Alysin Hauptner (Beth's former assistant and my business partner at No Tan Lines) and I got in my car. At some point I kicked Alysin out of the car and threw her briefcase out after her. I called Bo repeatedly and then abandoned the car. The police later found it with the back of the car left wide open and my purse in it.

After I banged on the door of strangers and was arrested, I was taken to jail. The police report shows that they called Beth, and instead of bailing me out, her reply was, "Take that drunk bitch to jail."

When I came to my senses the next morning I saw bars and knew immediately where I was but had no clue as to how I got there. A police officer eventually walked by and I said, "Excuse me, but why am I here?" After a brief answer when another officer walked by I said, "Excuse me, what happened?" Then I asked to use a phone.

I first called Beth, who said she was not going to come to get me. Maybe all the times I messed up had come rushing back to her and she wanted to wash her hands of me. Or not. In either case, I was so disappointed. I next called everyone I knew who had a bail license. It was afternoon before I found someone to bail me out, but before they arrived Beth had mobilized the *Dog the Bounty Hunter* camera crew and they were there to capture every humiliating second of my release.

The interesting thing about our news media is that they rarely tell the full story. With our attention span now down to nanoseconds, stories like mine get only partially told before the reporter moves on to something else. What the public was left with, unfortunately, was that I was out of control in the middle of the night, bothering strangers at their home, and was arrested.

Little, if anything, was said about my drink being drugged, and the end result was that I got a lot of mixed reactions from fans of the show. Some people sent me hate mail or posted terrible and untrue things about me online. But many others were supportive of the situation and of me. I'm glad I finally get to tell the full truth of the matter in this book, so I can put the incident to rest once and for all. I can definitely say it will never happen again, for I am now very careful about what I eat and drink, especially when I am in public.

After the arrest, Bo and I began going to go to church more regularly. We were already divorced, but we had vowed to be good parents together to our children. And for the most part, we are.

The first time we went the preacher told a three-part story about the shepherd and the lamb, a gold coin, and the prodigal son. All three stories were about the fact that God enjoys the return of lost sinners, and I felt exactly as the lamb must have when the shepherd, in a final attempt to stop the lamb from wandering off, broke its leg, forcing it to stay close. That's how I looked at my arrest. That was God "breaking my leg."

Another blessing is that I have tried in recent years to be a better sister to my brother Tucker. If I am at the bottom of the Chapman family totem pole, then Tucker sits right on my shoulders. From childhood he has been what others call a problem child. He was expelled from just about every school he ever attended and in seventh grade was thrown out for bringing a gun to school. By that time he was no longer allowed at Dad's because he stole too many things from him and Beth.

Tucker dropped out of school in the ninth grade and at age eighteen was arrested for armed robbery when he and several friends lured a Japanese tourist into his own hotel room, where they proceeded to tie him up and steal his things. The friends were caught right away, but Tucker, ever the bounty hunter's son, stayed on the run for about six months. He asked Dad for help, but when it came to Tucker, Dad had thrown up his hands long ago.

Tucker was eventually caught and served four years of a twenty-year sentence. He was released not too long after Barbara died and was out for several years. At first he tried. Dad gave him a job but had to fire him after Beth asked Tucker to return a client's cell phone case and he stole it instead. When Leland asked Tucker to vacuum the office Tucker only vacuumed one corner. As you can imagine, Tucker and Beth butted heads over just about everything, and he also had issues with Dad that went back to our childhood.

Bo even gave him a job, but had to let him go after Tucker didn't show up.

In October 2007 Tucker turned over a portion of an audiotaped conversation he had with Dad to the *National Enquirer*. In the full version of the conversation, Dad tried to get Tucker away from drugs and away from some people whom Dad felt were encouraging Tucker's drug use. Some of those people, including Tucker's girlfriend, happened to be black. In this private conversation, Dad used the n-word when talking about Tucker's friends. Tucker then made this private conversation public, and due to public outcry, A&E was forced to suspend production on the show.

Should Dad have used that terrible word? Of course not. He was angry with Tucker, and we all say things in anger that we shouldn't. Dad was very wrong, but so was Tucker.

I didn't speak to Tucker for about a year after that. I was too angry. Then one day in June 2009 Tucker called. He was in Waikiki and was supposed to meet his probation officer but he was too drugged up to get there. He wanted me to help, but I was hesitant. Finally I decided to call Bo and tell him what I was doing. If Bo didn't hear from me in an hour he could assume that Tucker had stolen my cell phone and car and he should call the police.

Tucker didn't want to meet his PO because he knew he would not pass his drug test. He also knew that all his chances were up and if he went back to prison, he'd stay there for a long, long time. His future looked so bleak, in fact, that just hours earlier Tucker had tried to overdose on heroin. Instead, he woke up in a pile of his own vomit.

I was shocked when I picked Tucker up. His eyes were hollow, his cheeks sunken, his hair unkempt and stringy. I took him home, fed him, and called his PO. After much negotiating and cajoling, I finally got Tucker to agree to meet with the woman, and of course the result of that meeting was that Tucker was led away in handcuffs.

Since then he has been imprisoned in Arizona and is doing as well as can be expected. To my knowledge he is off all the drugs and works out daily. The most recent picture I have of him shows him bulked up like Duane Lee. Our mother sends him a little money every week.

I talk to Tucker as often as I can, which isn't all that often, as he is not able to get to a phone regularly. But I believe that God wants me to give Tucker hope for his future, and that's what I try to do. I often think back to the story of the prodigal son and pray that someday Dad and Tucker will be reunited.

It won't be easy, however. Dad and Tucker have not spoken since the n-word incident. And our society does not offer enough support to released prisoners. Many of them, like Tucker, have never paid a phone bill, had a checking account, signed a lease or rental agreement, or done a monthly budget. They have no life skills and often return to prison because they do not have the knowledge needed to function in society.

Tucker's childhood was my childhood. He had many of the

same incidences of dysfunction that Barbara and I did. Barbara didn't make it, but I hope with everything I have that Tucker does.

★

Recently, I was also a strong advocate for my nephew Travis, when an audiotape that documented his abuse by his father made international headlines. In October 2011 we learned that Travis's dad had physically abused him, and it turned out there was an audiotape to prove it. This came after police and Child Protective Services had been notified that Travis Sr. was beating his son.

After Barbara passed, Travis stayed with me for a while and then with Dad and Beth. Later his dad told us he wanted to be part of his son's life, and our family was cautiously supportive of that. Travis Sr. had worked for Dad off and on for years, and gradually little Travis spent more and more time with his dad until he was there full-time.

We knew from the tape that Travis was being abused, and all we wanted to do was get him out of that terrible situation. The legal issues quickly turned into an international media circus. First Dad, Beth, and I were hit with a restraining order. Big Travis claimed falsely that we harassed him, accused him of beating his child, and slandered him. Well, we didn't harass him, and the second item was true, which made the last point moot.

We all ended up testifying at several court hearings, and when everything fell out, Dad was granted temporary custody of Travis, and Travis Sr. had to go to parenting classes. Big Travis was also allowed visits with his son.

Video of six or seven police cars descending upon Travis Sr.'s house to get little Travis was on the news for days. Travis is now doing well and loves being with the other kids in our family. I have to say that I am so blessed to have him in my life. It is like always having a little piece of Barbara with me.

In May 2012, as the eighth season was in the middle of airing, we got the news that A&E had canceled *Dog the Bounty Hunter*. I think we all knew it was coming; we just didn't know when. Not many shows run eight seasons, so we were very lucky in that respect.

The timing on news like that is never good, but Leland, Duane Lee, and I had all been flexing our wings for some time. Leland and Duane Lee are in their mid- and late thirties. They love our family very much, but are grown men who want to make their own mark in the world. And they will.

Dad and Beth also have lots of plans, some of which will probably be apparent by the time this book is published.

As for me, I look back on my life with a deep and powerful gratitude that I am alive and well, for I know how easily things could have turned out differently. I also have enough objectivity to realize that I do not want others to grow up as I did. I know others are out there suffering within dysfunctional families, living in families where one or more member is mentally ill, uses alcohol to excess, or takes hard drugs.

It all goes back to the cycle of abuse. It has to stop. It must stop. We need to teach people positive life skills so they can cope with the stresses of life productively. Without that, we all revert to the behavior we learned from watching the adults around us in our childhood. If they made poor choices, if they lived amid dysfunction, then it is likely that we will, too.

That's why I've formed the Proper Choice Foundation so I can show girls and other young women that they have choices. I also provide them with my very personal story of the dysfunction that surrounded me throughout my young life, and the improvements I have been able to make myself. I also hope the foundation can someday build a home for teen mothers that will teach them life skills and self-esteem. I do this knowing that if someone had done the same for me, it might have saved me a lot of heartache. This is my message and will be for the rest of my life. No one needs to live the life I did.

I have also opened with my business partner, Alysin Hauptner, a boutique salon on the east side of Oahu called No Tan Lines LLP. No Tan Lines is a traditional luxury tanning salon, but we also offer Red Light Anti-Aging Therapy. This exciting scientific discovery uses photo rejuvenation via red light technology as a natural, safe, and relaxing method that triggers your body to increase your own production of collagen. In turn, it smoothes and reduces fine lines to create more youthful-looking skin.

I met Alysin when she was Beth's assistant, and you also may have seen her on some episodes of *Dog the Bounty Hunter*. Off-camera we realized we both had the desire to help men and women feel good about themselves, and the salon was born.

Finally, I am working on a television project of my own. Hopefully you will already know more about it by the time you read this book, but for now, let's just say I am optimistic that I will be back on the air in an entirely new way very soon. I have surrounded myself with a wonderful and experienced team of people who are getting the job done, and I just know you are going to be inspired by this new project.

★

I also know with everything I have inside me that my battles with addiction will be lifelong. Between a genetic predisposition and my very dysfunctional childhood, addiction is like a ball of fire waiting to explode inside me. Right now I am winning the war, but I am realistic and know there is a possibility that the future may bring tough battles.

In closing, I have two things to ask. The first is that if you see people going off track, find a way to help. Talk to them and make a point to help them find positive choices and solutions. If someone had done that for me when I was young, my teen years could have been completely different. If someone had done that for Barbara, she might still be here today.

The second is that if you are surrounded by dysfunction, as I was, know there is a better way. Find a counselor, pastor, teacher, friend, neighbor—someone who will help you. It might not be the first person you ask, or the second, so don't give up. God will lead you toward help if you are open to it. You *do* matter; you *are* worth the effort. Your road may be long and hard, but the rewards will be huge for the rest of your life.

Wonderful things await you. I know. I've been there and I've come out on the other side. Wouldn't it be amazing if each of you could stop the cycle of abuse in your family? Just think what a collective difference we could make across the world. Years from now we could all live in peace and love and there wouldn't be a need for jobs such as bail bondsmen and bounty hunters.

While I've come to the end of my story so far, this really is only the beginning. I thank you so much for reading my book. If you've enjoyed it, I hope you will recommend it to others. If my story helps even one other person find his or her way, then all the trials I have lived through are worth it. Aloha oe'.